Making Lawn Ornaments In Wood

Complete Building Techniques & Patterns

Paul Meisel

FOX BOOKS

Fox Chapel Publishing Co Inc.

A Special Thanks

In 1983, my wife, Pat had the idea to market our project plans to hobbyist woodworkers. From the beginning, it was Pat who was in charge of personnel, taxes, insurance, accounting and all those things that keep a company going. She is the
person behind the scenes.

We both hope you enjoy this book of lawn ornament projects. I've enjoyed writing it, but I want to especially thank Pat whose hard work and support made this book possible. Many of our customers have told us how much they enjoy our woodworking plans. On their behalf, and with my utmost love, it is my pleasure to dedicate this book to Pat Meisel.

Paul Meisel, 1998

©1999 by Fox Chapel Publishing Company, Inc.

Publisher: Alan Giagnocavo
Project Editor: Ayleen Stellhorn

ISBN #1–56523–104–X

Making Lawn Ornaments in Wood: Complete Building Techniques & Patterns is a revised Second Edition of the work by the same name first published in 1995. Revisions include new patterns and a color mixing chart. The patterns contained herein are copyrighted by the author. Artists can make any number of projects based on these patterns. The patterns themselves, however, are not to be photocopied for resale or distribution under any circumstances. Any such copying is a violation of copyright laws.

To order your copy of this book,
please send check or money order
for $14.95 plus $2.50 to:
Fox Books Orders
1970 Broad Street
East Petersburg, PA 17520
1–800–457–9112

Try your favorite book supplier first!

Table of Contents

Introduction *1*

Chapter 1
The History of Lawn Ornaments *3*

Chapter 2
Selecting the Patterns *5*

Chapter 3
Choosing the Right Stock *7*

Chapter 4
Transferring the Pattern to Wood *13*

Chapter 5
Cutting the Project *21*

Chapter 6
Preparing the Wood for Paint *25*

Chapter 7
Selecting Paints & Brushes *37*

Chapter 8
Priming & Painting *43*

Chapter 9
Displaying Your Lawn Ornaments *51*

Pattern Section *57*

Introduction

While modern materials make it easier for today's hobbyist, the methods for building lawn ornaments have not changed dramatically in 90 years. Pine boards and lead based paints were used by builders at the turn of the century. Today, the availability of plywood, electric saws, better quality paints and more modern designs add to the pleasure of the do-it-yourselfer.

Unlike most woodworking projects, lawn ornaments must withstand the brutal effects of the harsh outdoor environment. Therefore the choice of materials and the proper application of the correct finish is extremely important. This book includes time proven building and painting techniques, as well as detailed information on plywood and paint selections.

CHAPTER 1

History of Lawn Ornaments

Though lawn ornaments seem to be unique to the United States, little has been written on their history.

Examples of plywood lawn ornaments approximately 30 years old. The owner, who lives in Minnesota, put them out only in summer. By placing them in a relatively protected area they lasted a very long time. The paint is now beginning to crack and blister.

Pine boards, three quarter inch to one inch thick, were used for home building in the late 1800's. The wide, relatively knot-free boards available at the time were the logical choice for lawn ornaments. Hobbyists could make projects up to 16 inches wide without having to glue up stock.

Plywood came into popular use in the 1940's. Exterior grades of plywood were introduced and proved themselves on such daring projects as the high speed PT (patrol torpedo) boats developed during World War II. After the war, plywood became more readily available to the do-it-yourselfer, and was found ideal for many applications. Plywood was a boon to do-it-yourselfers because it allowed much larger projects to be made without the need to glue up separate boards.

Today, both plywood and solid wood are used for lawn ornaments.

It is likely that do-it-yourself plans were sold in the early 1900's but any such plans would be very rare. (If readers know of such plans, please contact me. It would be interesting to include samples in the next reprint of this book.)

As woodworking became more popular for the do-it-yourselfer in the 1930's and 1940's, numerous plan companies began to appear. One company, *Home Workshop Patterns*, had well over 100 plans available to the do-it-yourselfer. Topics included bird houses, children's toys, furniture, knick knacks, whirligigs, and a number of different lawn ornaments. It is interesting to compare these early plans with the more modern designs which have been developed for this book.

Samples of Home Workshop Patterns **circa 1940's or 1950's.**

Woodworking as a hobby has tremendously increased in popularity in recent years. This interest has created an unprecedented demand for project plans of all types. Many purists love the older designs, such as those from the 1940's. These old fashioned lawn ornament designs do add a special touch to the outside appearance of older homes. Typical of these older, "traditional" design were dogs, forest animals and children.

The Flamingo Boom

During the 1920's, Florida became a very popular vacation spot. Tourists returned home with souvenirs of pink Flamingos. By the 1950's flamingos had become as much a part of middle-class America as crew-cuts and poodle skirts.

The first Flamingo lawn ornament was introduced in 1952 by the Union Plastics Company of Massachusetts. It proved successful enough that by 1957 a revised and more life-like version was introduced. Union Plastics is reported to have sold millions of these "atomic pink" plastic lawn flamingos during the following decade.

The popularity of lawn flamingos slowly died out by the 1970's. Then in 1983, *The New York Times* ran an article titled "Where Did All Those Flamingos Go?" Up went the sales again, with 450,000 sold in 1985.

With such a history, flamingos are likely to remain a natural choice for yard ornaments for generations to come. Patterns for flamingos are included in this book.

A plastic lawn flamingo.

The Yard Butt

In the 1980's, one new yard ornament design screamed into popularity. It was a simple design of a woman bending over in a polka-dot dress. Considered by many to reflect "middle-class" taste this lawn ornament, nevertheless, became extremely popular.

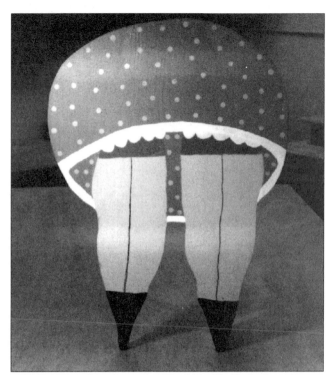

This woman bending over "Yard Butt" is likely the most popular yard ornament ever conceived.

If nothing else, the "woman bending over" was responsible for renewed interest in yard ornaments. Many people made money selling "yard butts" at craft shows and flea markets. Others made the projects for themselves.

At first people seemed content to simply place their plywood yard butt anywhere in the yard. Standing by itself it became a focal point. Next, a "man" yard butt was introduced and a type of "lawn grouping" was created.

New interest in lawn ornaments created a demand for more designs. Hundreds of different lawn ornament patterns were created in the last two decades. These plans, which are available from the Meisel Hardware Specialties mail order catalog, meet a large variety of interests. Patterns are available for forest animals, farm animals, child and adult figures, as well as for Easter, Halloween, Thanksgiving, Christmas, and other holidays.

This wide variety of patterns allows hobbyists the flexibility of grouping several different lawn ornaments together, thereby creating different yard scenes. This book shows dozens of examples of how compatible yard ornaments can be grouped together.

Readers are invited to send photographs of their own creations to the author for possible inclusion in the next printing of this book. Mail to Paul Meisel, P.O. Box 70, Mound, MN 55364. You can play a part in the next lawn ornament renaissance!

CHAPTER 2

Selecting the Patterns

In this book, you will find patterns for many different projects. While it may be tempting to select a single project to start with, it is best to select two or more projects so you will be able to display a "yard grouping". Look over the pictures of yard groupings in this chapter and first four pages in the color section starting on page 29. Pay attention to how each grouping would look in your yard. Are you going to decorate your wood pile? A choice of flowers, birds and squirrels would complement a wood pile nicely. Do you have a garden that you would like to perk up with color? A selection of wooden flowers, colorful birds and farm animals will enhance a flower or vegetable garden. Perhaps you would prefer a humorous scene, like the Boy being chased up a tree by the Climbing Dog.

Whether decorating a wood pile, a shed, a fence, a garden, or creating a scene in the grass, there are enough projects in this book to allow you to create dozens of different groupings. In addition to helping you decorate your lawn, this book provides tips and techniques. It is a "how-to" book which happens to include a good variety of introductory projects. Once you have made some of these projects, you may want to order additional patterns. Examples of some of the commercially available patterns are pictured in the full color section of this book. These plans can be ordered from the Meisel Hardware Specialties mail order catalog.

Lawn Ornaments as a Family Project

Unlike the more advanced woodworking hobbies of fine furniture making, wood carving or lathe turning, building lawn ornaments can be a family project. Children can participate in the early planning process by helping to select which figures will be used and how the figures will work together as part of the overall lawn grouping. After this initial planning, and with the children properly supervised, the whole family can help cut and paint the projects. After the lawn ornaments are completed, children can position these ornaments in the lawn to create the desired display.

The more family members that become involved the better. Besides increasing self-confidence, children will become more conscious of the whole notion of responsibility for maintaining property. They will also be more willing to periodically mow "their" lawn and reposition the yard ornaments in new and varied arrangements.

Flowers, birds and squirrels add decoration to this wood pile.

The Art of Arranging Groupings

One of the joys of lawn ornaments is that they can be easily rearranged to create totally different effects. The groupings are limited only by your imagination. Since projects which are mounted in the lawn must be removed each time the lawn is mowed, you always have a new opportunity to rearrange them. Create a new display each week! In the pictures below notice how three Running Geese are rearranged for many different effects.

"I'm sure it's over here somewhere."

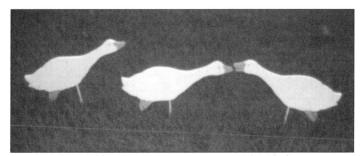

These friendly yard geese appear to be kissing.

"I'm over here!"

Feeding time for three yard geese.

"Does that water taste good?"

"The Great Chase"

"Bet you can't catch me!"

"What are you looking at?"

6

CHAPTER 3

Choosing the Right Stock

Softwood Boards

Lawn ornaments are typically made from either soft-wood boards or exterior type plywood. The three Running Geese which were displayed in various arrangements in the previous chapter were made from 3/4" thick softwood boards. Softwood boards are also the material of choice for the song birds and the flower projects in this book. Most any species of softwood lumber which you purchase at the lumber yard will be satisfactory for making the smaller lawn ornaments described above.

Avoid "finger jointed" stock. "Finger joining" is a method whereby short pieces of solid stock are joined end to end to make long pieces. This material is often knot free, but there is no guarantee that the glue used is of an exterior quality. If in doubt, it is best to avoid any material with an added potential to fail once it is in use. As a general rule, redwood, cedar, pine, and fir boards will all be satisfactory, assuming they are not plagued with knots, splits and sap streaks, or loaded with too much moisture. Before purchasing lumber, check to see that it is wide enough for the pattern. The running geese are about 4-3/4 inches wide. Be sure the stock you purchase is wide enough to fit the project.

Plywood

For larger projects, plywood is the logical choice. Care must be taken when selecting the plywood. There are many types of plywood panels which will work well for lawn ornaments. Your choice will be affected by both cost and availability. It is worth taking some time to review the choices that are available.

The American Plywood Association (APA) is a nonprofit trade association whose member mills produce approximately eighty percent of the structural wood panel products manufactured in the United States. The APA, together with the National Bureau of Standards and lumber producers, distributors, consumers and users, has established voluntary standards for grading and specifying lumber manufactured in the USA and Canada.

Exterior-type Plywood

The APA Standard classifies plywood panels into two types: interior and exterior. Interior-type plywood should not be used for lawn ornaments or any other projects which will be used outdoors. For lawn ornaments, only exterior-type plywood should be used. The APA defines Exterior-type plywood as plywood which will retain glue bond when repeatedly wetted and dried.

Understanding Plywood Veneer Grades

The term "grade" may refer to panel grade or to veneer grade. Panel grades for exterior plywood panels are generally identified in terms of the veneer grade used on the face and back of the panel (i.e. A-B, A-C, B-C, etc.).

Veneer grades define the appearance of the veneer. The highest quality veneer is "N" grade. "N" grade veneer is used in furniture grade plywood only, and therefore is not available in exterior plywood. "D" grade veneer is used only in panels intended for interior use or applications protected from permanent exposure to the weather. For exterior plywood, "A" veneer is the highest grade, and the lowest is "C".

Veneer Grade

Grade A Veneer - Must be firm, smoothly cut, and free of knots, pitch pockets, open splits, and other open defects. Synthetic fillers may be used to fill small cracks or checks. Up to 18 patches are permitted to repair veneers with knotholes or other defects.

Grade B Veneer - Must be solid and free from open defects and broken grain (except some small splits not wider than 1/32 inch, and horizontal or surface tunnels no more than 1/16 inch across, 1 inch in length, and up to 12 in number). Minor sanding and patching defects, including sander slips, shall not exceed five percent of panel area. Synthetic fillers may be used to fill small cracks or checks. Knots are permitted if they do not exceed 1 inch as measured across the grain. Knots must be sound and tight. Pitch streaks must not exceed 1 inch in width. Discolorations are permitted.

Grade C Veneer - Sanding defects that will not impair the strength or serviceability of the panel are permitted.

Knots must be tight and not more than 1/2 inch as measured across the grain. Open knotholes, usually not to exceed 1 inch, are permitted. Splits up to 1/2 inch in width by 1/2 panel length or 3/8 inch in width by any length are permitted.

Grade C Plugged Veneer - May contain knotholes and other open defects not larger than 1/4 inch by 1/2 inch. Sound and tight knots up to 1-1/2 inches measured across the grain, splits up to 1/8 inch wide, plugs and patches.

Exterior-Type Grades

Plywood is made from a combination of veneer sheets glued together with the grain direction of the layers at right angles to one another. A combination of grades of veneers may be used. For example, an "A" grade may be used on the front and a "C" grade on the inner plys and on the back. The chart below shows the standard combination of veneers which make up various grades for exterior type plywood panels, and shows which are recommended for lawn ornaments

Exterior-Type Grades

Panel Grade Designations	Minimum Veneer Quality			Recommendation for Lawn Ornaments
	Face	Back	Inner Plies	
Marine, A-A, A-B, B-B, HDO, MDO				excellent
Special Exterior, A-A, A-B, B-B, HDO, MDO				excellent
A-A	A	A	C	excellent
A-B	A	B	C	excellent
A-C	A	C	C	good
B-B (concrete form)				unsatisfactory
B-B	B	B	C	not recommended
B-C	B	C	C	not recommended
C-C Plugged	C Plugged	C	C	unsatisfactory
C-C	C	C	C	unsatisfactory
A-A High Density Overlay	A	A	C Plugged	excellent
B-B High Density Overlay	B	B	C Plugged	excellent
B-B High Density Concrete Form Overlay	B	B	C Plugged	not recommended

This abbreviated chart is based on information from the American Plywood Association (APA) and is shown only to illustrate the various types of plywood panels. For complete information contact the APA and request the booklet entitled US Product Standard PS 1-83.

APA Trademarks

Plywood manufactured in the United States by mills who are members of the American Plywood Association is identified by one of the APA's trademarks. These trademarks, part of APA Product Standard PS 1-83, are intended to provide for clear understanding between buyer and seller. As shown below, the stamp for sanded grades of plywood includes the following information: Veneer grade(s), species group number, exposure durability, mill number and product standard.

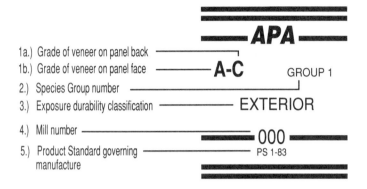

1a.) Grade of veneer on panel back
1b.) Grade of veneer on panel face
2.) Species Group number
3.) Exposure durability classification
4.) Mill number
5.) Product Standard governing manufacture

APA
A-C GROUP 1
EXTERIOR
000
PS 1-83

Sample of APA Trademark.

1a. & 1b. Veneer Grades

In the sample above, the grades are specified as "A" grade veneer on the face of the panel and "C" grade veneer on the back of the panel.

2. Species Group Number

The group number refers to specific categories of acceptable lumber species which may be used in the production of the panel. Group 1 includes certain types of Douglas Fir, Beech, Birch and other species.

3. Exposure Durability

This panel is classified as exterior type.

4. Mill Number

This is the identifying number of the mill who manufactured the plywood. All mills using this trademark are members of the APA.

5. Product Standard

This marking shows that the plywood has been produced in conformance of the U.S. Product Standard PS 1. This is a detailed performance standard developed in cooperation with the APA.

More about Exterior-type Plywood Panels

The chart on page 8 titled Exterior-Type Grades lists Marine grade, as well as HDO and MDO. These are all excellent grades of plywood to use for lawn ornaments.

A typical stamp as found on a plywood panel.

Marine Grade

Marine plywood panels are manufactured with the same glueline durability requirements as other exterior type panels, but with more restrictive veneer quality and manufacturing requirements. Because marine plywoods all use exterior glue and better grade veneers, they hold up exceptionally well outdoors. Common thicknesses are 1/4", 3/8" and 1/2". The 1/4" is too thin for use in lawn ornaments. The 3/8" is better, but not preferred. Marine plywood 1/2" thick is an excellent choice. Marine plywood is manufactured in the following grades: A-A, A-B and B-B.

MDO (Medium Density Overlay)

Though expensive, MDO plywood is perhaps the best choice for lawn ornaments. MDO plywood is manufactured by bonding a resin-treated fiber overlay to one or both sides of an exterior type plywood panel. The surface overlay of MDO board is smooth and generally opaque. Most manufacturers produce MDO with a wood-tone surface color.

HDO (High Density Overlay)

HDO plywood is similar in many ways to MDO. It is manufactured with a thermo-set resin-impregnated fiber surface bonded under heat and pressure to both sides of exterior plywood. It is even more durable than MDO, but also more expensive.

Both MDO and HDO boards are easy to work with, and are very water resistant when primed and painted properly. These products are commonly used for concrete forms, soffits and fascias, cabinets and built-ins, truck and trailer linings, and highway signs.

High Density Overlay (HDO) and Medium Density Overlay (MDO) are also considered Marine grade plywood.

Tip: Because commercial sign shops frequently use HDO and MDO panels for signs, you may wish to check with your local sign painter to see if you can purchase smaller "leftover" pieces at a reduced price. Smaller pieces will be ideal for many of the projects in this book. To find sign painters, check the Yellow Pages under Signs.

Some producers offer panels with a pre-primed surface. When cutting lawn ornaments from pre-primed MDO board, only the sawed edges will need to be primed. Seal edges with one or two coats of top quality primer. MDO in 4-by 8-foot sheets sells for about $40-45 in 1/2 inch thickness as of this printing. Other similar products may be available from your lumber yard. Since products vary with different lumber yards, MDO board will not be stocked at every lumber yard, but many yards will special order it for you. If you have difficulty finding a source, call around to several lumber yards or check with your local sign painter for advice on where you might be able to obtain it.

Concrete Form Panels

Plywood for concrete panels is usually oiled at the mill. The oil prevents the surface of this panel from being painted. It is therefore unsuitable for lawn ornaments.

APA Sanded Plywood, Exterior-Type

Almost every lumber yard carries exterior-type plywood in A-C grade. This is generally the lowest cost exterior-type panel suitable for lawn ornaments.

The "A" grade veneer used on the face of the panel is sanded and plugged. It is ready to prime. The "C" grade veneer used on the back of the panel will contain open knots and/or splits which will have to be filled.

The interior veneers are typically "C" grade. The open knot holes in "C" grade veneer result in occasional open voids along the edges of the plywood. These voids will have to be filled before priming.

A-C sanded plywood is widely used in a multitude of construction, industrial and do-it-yourself applications. These panels are made in a variety of thicknesses. Choose 1/2 inch for making lawn ornaments.

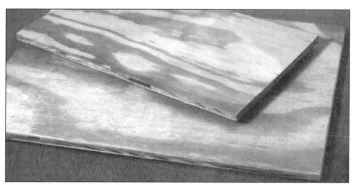

A-C grade exterior plywood.

Lauan Veneer Panels

In an effort to provide better quality plywood panels at an attractive price, some producers have begun to use Lauan as a face veneer over fir plywood.

Lauan trees (a Southeast Asia species) grow to a very large diameter and are straight and tall. As a result, Lauan veneers are smooth and relatively knot-free. When used as a top veneer over Douglas Fir plywood, an exterior rated panel with a very smooth surface is achieved. The back side of the plywood may be rough (typically grade C) and so will require some preparation prior to painting.

The photograph below shows the face side of an exterior plywood panel with a face veneer of Lauan. The face veneer is completely knot free. The inner veneers and back are Grade C Douglas Fir. Lauan has become more popular as supplies of mature Douglas Fir trees continue to diminish.

Fir plywood with a Lauan face veneer.

Preservative-Treated Plywood

Plywood which has been treated under pressure with the wood preservative Chromated Copper Arsenate can be used for lawn ornaments, but it is not preferred. This plywood, usually green in color, often has a great deal of moisture left from the treating process. Too much moisture will cause the paint to blister within a short time. If preservative treated plywood is used, it may be necessary to allow time for excess moisture to evaporate before cutting and painting the project.

There are other problems with using preservative-treated plywood. From a safety standpoint, EPA (Environmental Protection Agency) guidelines state that the preservative must be chemically affixed to the wood in a manner that makes it resistant to leeching (coming out of the wood and into your skin). We are told that, assuming that the preservative has been applied properly, it is not considered a particular danger for most people, especially after the wood has been exposed to the outdoors for a couple of months. Presumably this means without paint or other finish.

If you do use treated plywood, the EPA states that the following precautions should be taken:
1) Avoid skin contact. Wear gloves, a long-sleeved shirt, and a dust mask when handling and sawing treated lumber.
2) Dispose of sawdust and scrap wood in an appropriate manner. Never burn sawdust or scrap wood.

Imported Plywood - Finnish Birch

Finnish birch is a very high quality plywood manufactured in Finland. It is ideal for yard ornaments because it has very smooth surfaces, few if any interior voids, and it is made with waterproof glue.

The grade system used for Finnish birch is slightly different than with American plywoods. The grade sold by Meisel Hardware Specialties is S/BB. The grading scale is as follows:

S Grade Veneer - Very high quality veneer. Generally no open defects. No patches allowed. (Similar to the American Standard of Grade N.)

BB Grade Veneer - Knots and open defects in BB face veneers have been patched with small oval or round plugs (patches) before gluing.

NOTE: Do not confuse Finnish Birch plywood with Baltic Birch plywood which looks almost identical. Baltic Birch is generally more readily available in lumber yards because it is preferred by many cabinet makers for making drawers and cabinet interiors. It has very smooth surface veneers and good overall strength and durability. However, Baltic Birch is not manufactured with waterproof glue and therefore should not be used for projects intended for outdoor use.

Finnish Birch plywood can be purchased from Meisel Hardware Specialties. It is available by mail-order in 24 inch by 24 inch pieces. This size is large enough for many, but not all, of the lawn ornament projects in this book.

Finnish Birch Plywood

Types of Paneling to Avoid

There are several materials which, although readily available, should be avoided. They have not been found to be satisfactory for lawn ornaments and are not recommended.

Hardboard - Even the better quality "tempered" hardboard does not hold up well outdoors.

Particleboard - It has a generally smooth surface, but does not hold up well outdoors.

Waferboard - Some brands can be used outdoors, but these panels have a rough surface.

This photograph shows, from left to right, tempered hardboard, particleboard, and waferboard. These panels are not recommended for the projects in this book.

A Final Word on Plywood Choice

Always use the best quality plywood you can reasonably afford. Better grades of plywood, though initially more expensive to purchase, will save time, money and labor because they will need less preparation. These plywood grades will also result in longer project life. If you can't find quality plywood at your local lumber yard, ask if they can special order panels for you.

CHAPTER 4

Transferring the Pattern to Wood

Once you have selected patterns and purchased your plywood or solid stock, it is time to transfer the pattern to the wood. All of the patterns in this book are drawn **FULL SIZE**. Many patterns, such as the birds and flowers fit on a single page. For larger projects, two or more pages will need to be combined. There are two ways to use the patterns from the book.

Method 1
Paper Patterns

Remove the pages from the book (or photocopy them if you prefer to keep the book intact). For patterns that require two or more pages to be combined, trim the adjoining borders away and assemble the pages with tape.

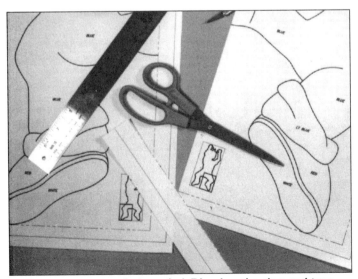

These pages were photocopied. Trim along borders and tape together.

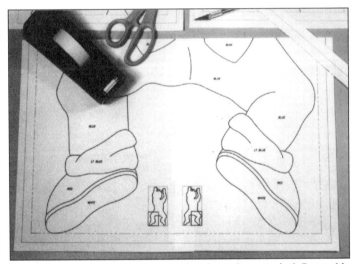

Pages can be either torn out of the book or photocopied. For multiple page patterns, the adjoining borders are trimmed and taped together.

Method 2
Polyethylene Transfers ("Poly Patterns")

To make a more durable "poly pattern", trace the patterns from the book to a large piece of polyethylene plastic with a felt tip marker. Making a poly pattern may seem like an extra step at first, but there are some real advantages.

First, natural polyethylene plastic film is semi-transparent. This makes it easy to align and trace each page of a multiple page pattern. Second, since you can see through a poly pattern, it is much easier to position the pattern on your wood. You can look through the poly film to see any lumber defects, such as knots and avoid them. Third, you can arrange multiple patterns more tightly, which reduces waste.

Another advantage is that the direction the pattern faces can be changed. For example, if you want two of the same dog facing each other, simply use the poly pattern and carbon paper to transfer the first dog image to your wood. Then flip the poly pattern over and transfer the "reversed" image to your wood.

Low cost Polyethylene Plastic Film works well for making durable one piece patterns. This roll is 3-1/2 mils thick. Other thicknesses can also be used.

This pattern was traced from the book to polyethylene plastic.

Another advantage of using a poly pattern is that you need only to flip the poly pattern over to transfer interior lines to the *back* of your project. This is a great convenience if you are painting details on both the front and back of the wood. Save your poly patterns. They are very durable and will last for years.

Polyethylene plastic film is available at hardware stores. It comes packaged in different sheet sizes and weights (thicknesses). The thickness is measured in "mils". A mil is one-thousandth of an inch. A good thickness is 3-1/2 mil (or 3-1/2 thousandths of an inch). The roll pictured contains a 100 x 25 foot sheet of 3-1/2 mil natural-colored polyethylene plastic. This may seem like too large of a roll to purchase just for making patterns, but it is very inexpensive (around four dollars) and there are other uses for the poly. For example, use it as a drop cloth to protect the floor when painting lawn ornaments or use it to wrap seasonal lawn ornaments when storing them.

Marking the Poly

A medium point *permanent* ink felt tip marker works best for marking the film. (Polyethylene has a "waxy" feel and the ink in *water-based* felt pens will "bead up" and not adhere well.) A ball point pen can also be used, but a felt tip marker with permanent ink is preferred.

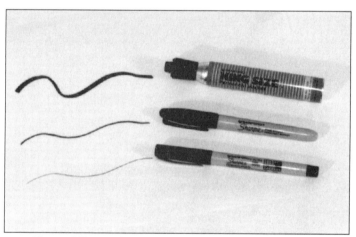

Three different sizes of permanent ink felt tip markers. The medium point (center) is preferred for making poly patterns.

Cutting the Poly to Size

For the six page pattern of the Boy Climbing it will be necessary to cut a piece of polyethylene approximately 20"x35". Mark a piece this size with a yardstick and felt tip marker and cut to size with a scissors.

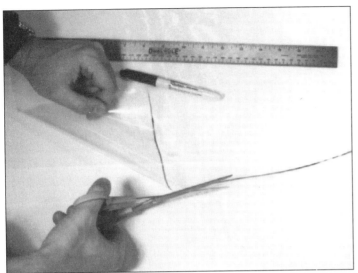

A 20"x 35" piece of poly plastic will
be large enough to trace a six page pattern.

Positioning the Poly

For clarity, positioning guides are provided for multiple page patterns. This makes it easier to see where each section of the pattern fits in relation to the other pages of that pattern.

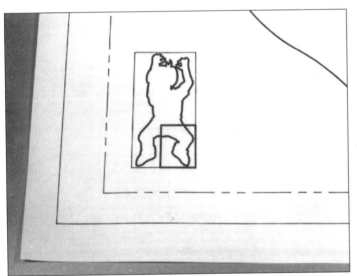

For large patterns where two or more pages must be combined, a positioning guide is included. This guide will show you how many pages must be combined and where each page is positioned.

Marking the Pattern

Position the polyethylene film and trace the first page of the pattern.

Transferring the first page of a
multipage pattern to the polyethylene film.

Next, move the poly to an adjoining page, align, and transfer that section. Continue this process until the entire pattern is traced.

The polyethylene sheet is aligned on an adjoining
page, then traced with the medium felt tip marker.

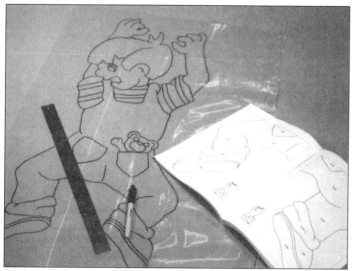

This completed poly pattern can be used over and over.

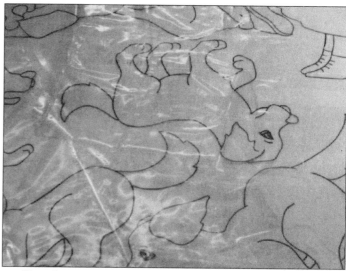

Six poly patterns have been positioned for the best yield.

Transferring Patterns to the Plywood

Since you will be working with large sheets of plywood, you may want to use saw horses and "2x4" supports to make a handy table for layout and cutting.

Tape all poly patterns to one another where they overlap. Then secure the poly pattern assembly to one side of the wood with tape or thumb tacks.

Saw horses with "2x4s" create a support for large plywood sheets.

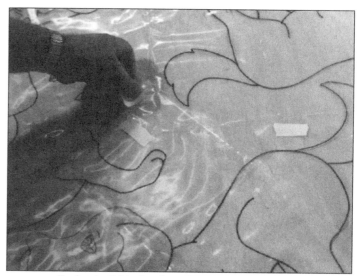

Taping individual poly patterns to one another.

Positioning Patterns on the Plywood

One advantage to preplanning an entire yard scene is that you can position all patterns on the plywood for the most efficient arrangement. Take time to move the patterns this way and that to determine the most efficient use of the plywood.

Tracing Patterns to Plywood

Slide carbon paper under one pattern at a time (ink side of carbon paper toward wood). Use a ball point pen to transfer the pattern to the plywood. A ball point rolls over the poly film more easily than a lead pencil. It is not necessary that the ink from the ball point is actually transferred to the poly film. It is only important that the pressure forces the pattern image through the carbon paper and onto the plywood. Transfer all inside and outside lines from the pattern at this time.

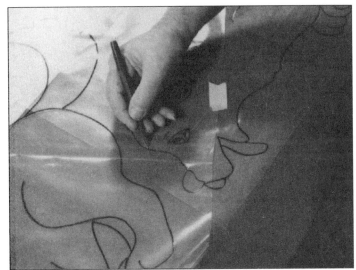

Transfer all inside and outside lines from the pattern onto the wood, using carbon paper and a ball point pen.

Continue to transfer other patterns to the wood in the same manner.

Marking Interior Lines

When you transfer the pattern to the plywood on any project, don't forget to transfer the interior lines. You will be retracing the interior lines with a blue ball point pen after the project is cut out. The ink from the ball point pen will bleed through the primer (even stain-blocking primer). The bleed through is very helpful because you can clearly see where to paint the various colors of the top coat.

Using Larger Blueprints

Lawn ornaments larger than those included in this book are available to the hobbyist. Meisel Hardware Specialties offers over 200 such plans. Once you have built some of the projects in this book, you will likely be anxious to try some new designs.

The same basic steps apply to making larger yard ornaments. Because they are drawn full size, the pattern sheets for these larger ornaments are big - as large as 42" x 96". Unless you have a large shop, it is easier to work on these projects outdoors or in a garage.

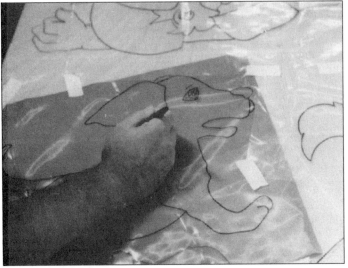

Transferring the next pattern to the wood.

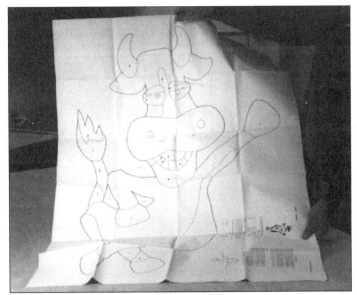

An example of a large lawn ornament plan. The full size patterns may be transferred directly to plywood using carbon paper. You may prefer to make a poly pattern before starting.

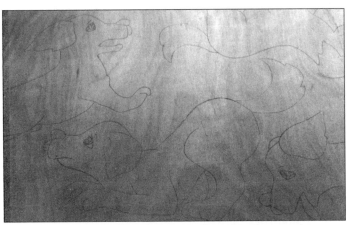

All six patterns have been transferred to the wood.

Place the plywood on the supports and begin the process of transferring the full size patterns. Multiple sheets of carbon paper are taped to the plywood and the project pattern is taped or pinned in place.

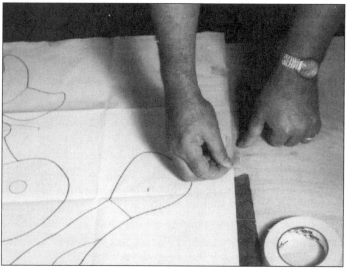

Taping a large paper pattern to the wood.

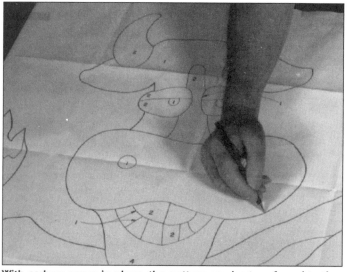

With carbon paper in place, the pattern can be transferred to the wood using a pencil or a pen.

In the photographs above, the pattern was transferred directly to the plywood with carbon paper. You may wish instead to make a poly pattern.

Poly pattern of Leaning Cow. Carbon paper will be placed under the poly pattern when transferring.

Transferring Patterns to Solid Wood Stock

Smaller projects such as Running Geese, Yard Birds and Yard Flowers, are best cut from 3/4" softwood boards. Pine, fir, cedar and redwood are all good choices.

Try to position the patterns *with* the direction of the wood grain, when possible. Also, avoid knots, splits and other defects.

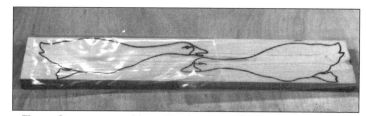

These Geese are positioned in the same direction as the wood grain. The poly pattern makes it easy to arrange the patterns and eliminates the chance of accidental overlapping.

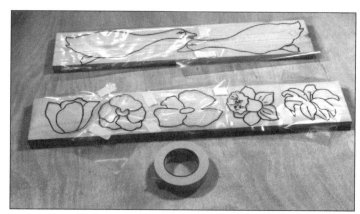

Patterns are taped down to solid wood in the same manner as with plywood.

Slide carbon paper under the poly
pattern and begin tracing the patterns.

Trace all the patterns before cutting.

If this project had been laid out with the grain running the length
of the tail, the spoilage may not have occurred.

CHAPTER 5

Cutting the Project

Jigsaws

All projects in this book can be made with an ordinary hand-held jigsaw (sometimes referred to as a sabre saw). These easy-to-use saws are available in a wide price range, (from about $40 to $200 as of this writing). The lower priced jigsaws are satisfactory, provided they are fitted with the correct blade. More expensive saws offer some advantages, such as reduced vibration, variable speed, or other convenient features. As a general rule, the more expensive the saw the more pleasurable it is to use, but it should be noted that you absolutely do not need a $200 jigsaw to make lawn ornaments. What is most important is using the proper saw blade and taking a little time to practice using the saw before cutting your project.

Jig Saw Blades

The best blade for cutting plywood has the teeth ground at alternating angles (rather than the more common "face ground" teeth). These "shark tooth" shaped teeth are ground to points like equilateral triangles, which cut on both the upward and the downward strokes. In addition, the blade is ground on both sides so the back of the blade is thinner than the front. This reduces binding and friction and eliminates burning of the wood.

"Sawtooth" blades are made only in Switzerland. Fortunately they are carried by several American hardware chains. They are available in one size only - 19 teeth per inch. You may be able to find them at your local hardware store, or you can purchase them from Meisel Hardware Specialties mail order catalog (Part #1335).

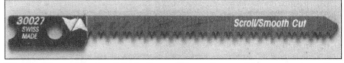

The preferred jigsaw blade for cutting plywood lawn ornaments.

Satisfactory results can also be obtained with "standard" jigsaw blades. Choose a fine tooth blade designated for use on plywood.

A Jigsaw is the most popular saw for plywood lawn ornaments.

Band Saws and Scroll Saws

Smaller projects may be cut on a band saw or scroll saw.

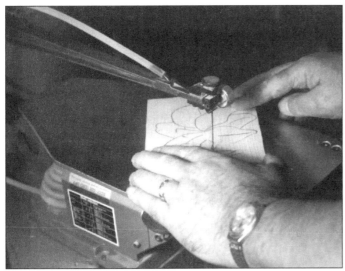

A scroll saw is preferred for small projects.

Band saws can be used for perimeter cuts on small or medium-sized lawn ornaments. Bandsaws cannot be used for inside cuts.

Practice Cutting

Before cutting your first project, practice cutting curves on scrap stock. You will soon get a feel for how the blade cuts. Check out how sharp the blade will turn. Getting used to the saw, the blade, and the wood which you will be using will result in a better job.

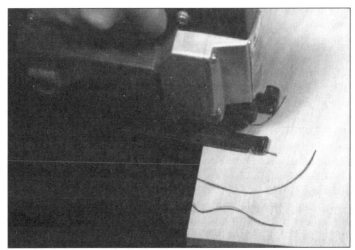

Before you start to cut the actual pattern, draw some curved lines in the scrap area of the wood and practice making cuts.

Interior Detail

Cut interior details first. On the Running Dog pattern, an area of the plywood must be removed where the legs cross. Before cutting, drill three 1/4" holes in this interior area. The holes are necessary to start the jig saw blade. Drilling two or more holes simplifies turning the blade in tight corners. Use caution when drilling to avoid splintering the back of the plywood.

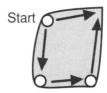

Start

This diagram shows drilling and cutting procedures for the interior area to be removed from the Running Dog project. Drill 1/4" dia. holes in all tight radius corners, then cut toward the sharp upper right corner from two directions.

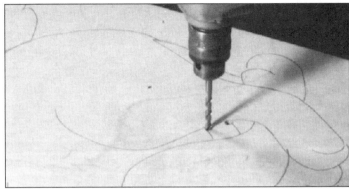

Starter holes are drilled where interior area must be removed.

Starting with the holes drilled on the
inside curves, saw toward any sharp corners.

After the interior section has been cut away, proceed to saw around the perimeter of the pattern.

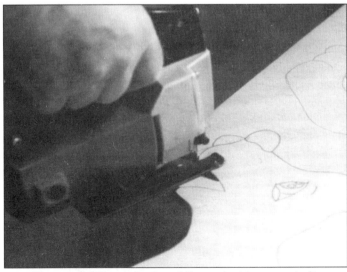

Saw around the perimeter of the project to separate it
from the plywood panel. Cut around details such as the dog's
mouth for now. It will be easier to finish the details after
the project has been separated from the plywood.

CHAPTER 6

Preparing the Wood for Paint

Filling Surface Irregularities

For projects which will be viewed from both sides, you will want to take time to properly fill any defects on both the front and back surfaces before applying the first coat of primer.

Choosing a Wood Filler

Because lawn ornaments are normally displayed outdoors, choose a water-proof wood filler. Avoid fillers designed for interior use only.

Applying Wood Filler

Use a putty knife to apply the wood filler. Put a little filler on the putty knife and push it down into the split, hole or rough surface. Smooth off the top by pulling the knife across the surface towards you. Form a slight mound with the filler so that if it shrinks while drying, it will not leave a hollow dip. Once spread, it is best not to manipulate the filler more than necessary. In some cases, especially if large voids are being filled, shrinkage will necessitate a second application of filler. Don't forget to fill voids in the edges of the plywood. This will help prevent moisture from getting at the interior veneers.

This wood filler is formulated for use outdoors.

Applying wood filler with a putty knife.

Expect shrinkage when filling larger voids.
A second coat may be required.

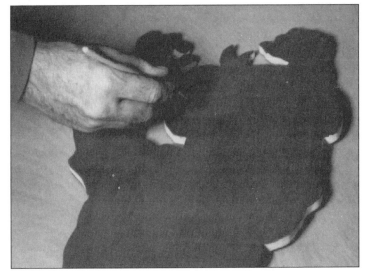

Since the back of this "Boy Climbing" lawn
ornament will not be seen, it was first primed, then
painted brown to blend in with the color of the tree trunk.

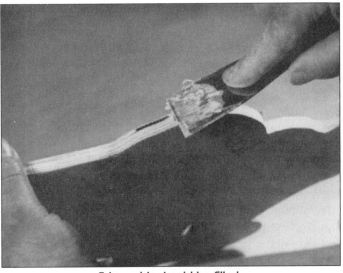

Edge voids should be filled.

When the Back Will Not be Viewed

Yard ornaments are often positioned so they are viewed from the front side only. In cases where the back will not be seen, there is no need to spend a great deal of time filling the splits, knot holes or other surface defects on the back. For these projects, it will be adequate to paint one or two coats of primer on the back, and perhaps a coat of the most dominant color.

Sanding Safety

Whether sanding by hand or using a power sander, always pay attention to safety. Consider who else will be affected by the dust you are creating. Even if the sanding dust doesn't bother you, what about others living in your home? Do any of these people have allergies to sanding dust? What about the neighbors? Is the dust blowing next door? Here are some safety tips:

• **Always wear safety glasses or other eye protection.** Wood dust, or worse - abrasive particles from the sandpaper, are very small and tend to become airborne. They can easily get in the eyes. They are not easily removed!

• **Wear proper dress.** A hat, an old shirt and pants, or a full-length shop coat are highly recommended. Why? Because you can remove them after sanding. Otherwise sanding dust remains on your clothes and hours later can get into the living room furniture and even into your eyes.

• **Wear a particle mask.** These low cost filters cover the nose and mouth. They are not uncomfortable to wear and they prevent sanding dust from entering the nasal passages, throat, and lungs.

• **Earplugs.** Advisable if doing a lot of machine sanding if excess noise causes discomfort.

Sanding the Filler

Filler sands quite rapidly. Use 100 grit abrasive paper wrapped around a block of wood.

Tip: A handy sanding block can be made from a 3" wide piece of 3/4" pine. Radius the ends and experiment to get the best length to fit a standard length sanding belt. For the 3" x 21" sanding belt pictured, a 10" long board was used.

Left: This block is made just long enough to fit a sanding belt from a belt sander. Right: A scrap of wood with a partial sheet of sand paper wapped around it. Either method provides a convenient way to hand sand the wood filler flat in preparation for the primer.

Sanding the filler with a sanding block.

Smoothing the Edges

The correct saw blade will leave a smooth edge which will normally need little or no sanding. If you experience any burning of the edge grain it it should be sanded enough to help assure good paint adhesion.

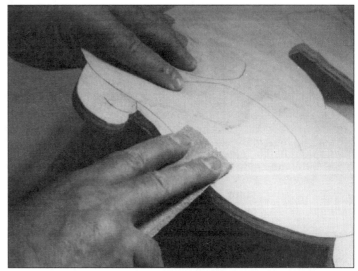

Sand burn marks or rough saw marks with 100 grit sandpaper.

Should You Round the Edges?

Although many believe that rounding the edges of the lawn ornament with a router and round over bit improves the appearance, rounding is not recommended for two reasons: First, more of the plywood edge is exposed. This increases the chance of moisture entering the plywood and makes it more difficult to fill any voids in the interior veneers, not to mention the added tear-out caused by the router bit. Second, it is very difficult to add outline highlights (using a paint marker) when the edges have been rounded over. (See the section on using paint markers in Chapter 8.)

Here is a sampling of the new patterns that were added during the most recent reprinting of this book.

Yard Birds

Scarecrow

Uncle Sam

Robby Raccoon

Yard Flowers

Hi/Bye Critters, Dog

Hi/Bye Critters, Bunny

Hi/Bye Critters, Duck

The following eight pages show how projects made from the lawn ornament patterns in this book can be arranged to create a wide variety of lawn groupings.

The Little Farmer Girl with Yard Geese,
Yard Birds and Yard Flowers.

There is plenty of activity in this yard.

A decorated wood pile.

Standing Dog meets Calico Hen and Chicks.

By substituting the Sniffing Dog, a completely different effect is created.

Traditional Flamingos. Use your imagination to decorate them, as shown below.

Cowboy Flamingos.

Holstein Cow Flamingos.

The Climbing Boy can be chased up a tree by the Climbing Dog, the Running Goose, or by other figures.

Separate arms and legs were attached to these Feeding Squirrels to create a way to hold a sign.

Feeding Squirrel and Sniffing Dog.

Running Cat chasing the Running Squirrel.

Running Goose chasing the Running Squirrel.

A different effect is created with the Squirrel running either up or down the tree.

Running Goose meets Sniffing Dog.

The Running Cat could just as
easily be chasing the Running Dog.

Another chase.

Lots of chasing going on!

A nicely decorated corner of the garden.

You can easily substitute the Barnyard
Chickens for the Yard Geese.

These examples show the wide variety of lawn ornament projects you can make to decorate your yard. Plans for these projects are available from the Meisel Hardware Specialties mail order catalog. To request a catalog, call 1-800-441-9870 or write to: Meisel Hardware Specialties, P.O. Box 70, Mound, Minnesota, 55364.

#W1082 Easter Cross Plan   #W1029 Baby Chicks Plan
#W1113 Powder Puff Rabbit Plan

#W927 Turkey and Pheasant Plan
#W886 Pilgrim Pals Plan Set

#W929 Scarecrow and Crows Plan

#W572 Pee Wee Pete Plan

#W859 Cats, Cats, Cats Plan Set

#W1516 Hardly A Cycle Plan

#W1285 Dinosaur Plan Set

#W1272 Beagle Welcome Plan

#W1252 Fire Hose Dalmatian Plan

33

#W507 Bloomin' Beulah Plan   #W508 Mad Max Plan

#W1521 Boy Running Plan   #W1522 Goat Running Plan

#W504 Mushroom Mama Plan
#W840 Hound and Fire Hydrant Plan

#W1565 Large Lucy Plan
#W1566 White Leg Larry Plan

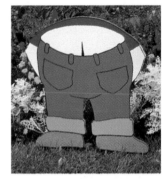

#W1270 Droopy Drawers Plan

#W1127 Boy and Dog Plan

#W1268 Humpty Dumpty Plan

#W1052 Robby Raccoon Plan
#W1116 Coon Hound Plan

#W1271 Tumbling Tommy Plan

#W1278 Wee Willie Plan

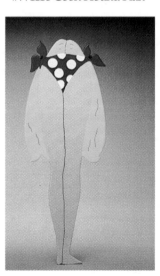

#W583 Leona Long Legs Plan

34

#W1230 Santa, Sleigh and Holsteins Plan Set

#W979 Candyland House Plan
#W974 Busy Elves Plan

#W1380 Post Office Plan
#W969 Santa's List Plan

#W1382 Rearview Deer Plan
#W1383 Outhouse Plan

#W954 Kenguin Penguin Plan
#W968 Candy Cane Plan
#W975 Toy Soldier Plan

#W760 Leaning Snowman Plan

#W645 Leaning Rudy Plan

#W1385 Droopy Drawers Santa Plan

#W283 Yard Size Nativity Plan Set

#W1404 Santa Welcome Plan

#W1010 Farmerboy Scarecrow Plan
and Calico Hen & Chicks (from this book)

#W695 Deer Family Plan Set

Cub from #W692 Bear Family Plan Set
and Running Squirrel (from this book)

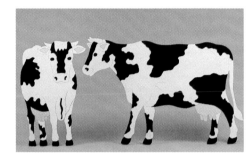

#W1323 Swinging Holsteins Plan Set

#W575 Sitting Bull Plan

#W235 Yard Cows Plan Set

#W573 Leaning Bull Plan   #W574 Leaning Heifer Plan

#W1094 Bessy n' Baby Plan Set
and Yard Flowers (from this book)

#W1052 Robby Raccoon Plan   #W1100 Mrs. Bruin's Family Plan Set
Large Bear from #W691 Bear Family Plan Set

#W839 Sea Birds Plan Set   #W841 Shark Alert Plan
#W1102 Fern, Fritz and Fonz Frogs Plan Set

#W838 Barnyard Chickens Plan   #W698 Sow and Piglets Plan

CHAPTER 7

Selecting Paints & Brushes

Effects of Outdoor Exposure

The harsh effects of outdoor weather are very damaging to wood and paint. It is essential to prepare the surface properly and choose the best primer and paint available. The three most damaging effects to outdoor projects are Ultraviolet (UV) radiation, moisture, and change in temperature.

Sunlight and UV Radiation

Direct sunshine can degrade the binder and pigment of a paint. Note: Binder is the additive in paint that helps it adhere to the surface being painted. Pigment is the material used for coloring the paint. Degradation caused by the sun can result in chalking (a white, chalky dust) and loss of color. While all grades of paint suffer these effects to some degree, lower quality paints (and interior paints) will generally fail much earlier than quality exterior paints.

The binders in latex paint tend to resist the effects of direct sunlight better than binders in oil-based paints. The reason is that the binders used in latex paints tend to be "transparent" to UV radiation, while oil binders actually absorb the radiation, which tends to break them down. Red and yellow paint colors are especially vulnerable to fading from UV radiation.

Water and Moisture

Moisture is especially hard on exterior paint. The source of the moisture can be rain, snow, dew, lawn sprinklers, condensation, and humidity from the substrate (the plywood or wood boards). As with UV radiation, moisture tests the paint's resistance to chalking and tint loss. Better grades of latex paints help fight these problems better than oil-based paints. This is primarily due to the characteristics of the binders they contain.

Water and moisture can also cause blistering of the paint. When wood gets wet, it expands. When the wood dries it contracts. Expansion and contraction of the wood puts great stress on the paint, and can result in cracking and flaking.

Latex paint is permeable ("breathable") and allows the water to vaporize and escape. High quality latex paints are very flexible, offering added protection against problems with cracking and flaking. Never attempt to paint wood that has a high moisture content. Allow wet wood to dry first.

Temperature Changes

Quite naturally, changes in temperature occur to a much greater degree out-of-doors than they do indoors. Like moisture, temperature changes cause the wood to expand and contract. This puts added stress on the paint.

Quality paints that offer both superior adhesion and flexibility help prevent cracking and flaking. Top quality acrylic latex paint is an especially good choice for exterior applications in areas where there are many heavy freeze-thaw cycles. The acrylic binder that is found in these paints is very durable and offers great flexibility.

Performance Characteristics

Desirable characteristics of good quality exterior paint include better color retention, resistance to chalking, resistance to blistering, and resistance to cracking and flaking.

Color Retention (Tint Retention)

Color retention is the capability of the paint to maintain

its color over time. The term applies only to tinted paints or factory colors, not to white paints.

A variety of factors can contribute to color loss in exterior paints. One common cause is deterioration of the paint, often due to binder breakdown, which can result in chalking and a whitening of the surface of the paint. The color itself can also break down. Organic pigments such as bright reds and yellows are most prone to this. Inorganic colors like red oxides and brown earth tones usually retain their color very well. Exposure direction can have a significant impact, too. Southern exposure gets the most direct sunshine and, thus, has the greatest tendency for color loss. Northern exposure is typically affected least by this problem. Quality latex exterior paints have better color retention than oil-based exterior paints.

Chalking

The term "chalking" refers to the formation of a white, chalky powder on the surface of the paint film. This condition often occurs as the binder is slowly degraded by sunshine and moisture. Over time, nearly all paints will show some chalking when they are subject to outdoor exposure. However, chalking is especially prevalent with flat paints and white or very light-colored paints. A low degree of chalking is often beneficial in whites and off-whites, since it tends to rid the surface of a certain amount of dirt and mildew. But excessive chalking is detrimental.

Excessive chalking can harm a paint job in three ways: it can result in chalk "run-down," which can deface the appearance of the surface below the painted area; it can lighten the color of the paint; and it can erode the paint film resulting in a loss of protection. Quality exterior latex paints are formulated to resist chalking so well, in fact, that it may not occur at all for several years. In order to keep the paint clean-looking, these paints often are designed to have excellent dirt resistance. This means that airborne dirt will not stick to the surface.

Blistering

Blistering is the formation of rounded "bubbles" of paint film. The cause is almost always moisture related. It will occur in lawn ornaments if the paint is applied to wood that has too high of a moisture content. Often just placing the plywood or solid wood stock in a dry area for several days before painting will be all that is necessary to allow the moisture to escape. This can occasionally be a problem in areas where the humidity is very high. The solution may be as simple as bringing the cutout pieces indoors where the humidity may be less due to better climate control (air conditioning).

The problems of blistering are more common in oil-based paints due to the vapor barrier that forms as they dry, trapping moisture beneath the paint. As the paint dries, the moisture will escape, lifting the paint off the wood as it evaporates. Latex paint, however, is more permeable. It allows a small amount of water vapor to pass through as it dries and greatly reduces the chance for blisters to form.

Blistering, followed by peeling, can also be caused by applying paint in very cold weather or very hot or windy weather. These extreme weather conditions cause the paint to dry too quickly.

Cracking and Flaking

Cracking and ultimately flaking of paint can occur for a variety of reasons. The paint may have inadequate adhesion and flexibility (common problems with lower quality paints). Cracking and flaking can also result when paint is applied in too thin a film. This can happen when paint is applied at a higher-than-recommended spread rate (overspread) or if the paint is thinned too much. These practices tend to diminish the paint's final film thickness, so that it is more vulnerable to cracking and flaking. Inadequate surface preparation can also cause these failures, especially when paint is applied to bare wood or a very porous surface without first applying a primer. A primer will provide better adhesion and will seal the surface, allowing the top coats of paint to perform properly.

Choosing the Best Primer and Paint

A primer is defined as a paint coating designed to form a film upon which a succeeding finish coat (or coats) of paint may be applied. Since the outdoor environment places tremendous demands on paint, always purchase the best grade of primer and paint you can reasonably afford.

Stain Blocking Primers

Stain blocking primers are formulated to prevent stain bleed-through. Stain bleed-through is a brownish or tan discoloration of latex paint that can occur when the paint is applied over certain types of bare wood. Naturally, it can be quite unsightly on white or light-colored paints. Stain bleed-through commonly occurs when tannin found in some kinds of wood, particularly cedar, redwood and mahogany, seep through latex paint and discolor it. Tannin, also called Tannic Acid, is a yellowish substance that bleeds from certain woods. Stain bleed-through can also occur when knots or sap streaks are painted over in any species of wood, including, of course, fir plywood. To avoid stain bleed-through, bare wood should be primed with a stain-resistant primer. Even though these primers may themselves become stained, they will keep the wood tannin from bleeding into the topcoat, except in the most severe cases.

The primer's stain-resistant property should be noted on the label or in the manufacturer's literature. For maximum protection, two coats of primer should be applied. These primers are specially formulated so that they will block the staining materials which leach out from the wood. Stain blocking primers typically contain a high binder to pigment ratio, zinc oxide or other pigments that block stains, and thickeners that help the primer form a stain-resistant film. Watch that you purchase a product that is suitable for outdoor use.

The most common stain-blocking primers are manufactured by Wm. Zinsser & Co. Inc. and Masterchem Industries. Zinsser offers four different stain-blocking primers: H$_2$OIL BASE, Bulls Eye 1•2•3, Kover-Stain and B-I-N. The first two are recommended for lawn ornaments. H$_2$OIL BASE and Bulls Eye 1•2•3 are exceptionally user friendly in that soap and water can be used to clean hands and brushes. Caution: B-I-N is not recommended for plywood because it dries to form a rigid film. It can therefore crack when weather causes the plywood to expand and contract. B-I-N *is* satisfactory for spot priming knots and splits. Masterchem offers KILZ2 and KILZ TOTAL ONE. Both of these products are satisfactory for priming lawn ornament projects, and both feature soap and water clean up.

For lawn ornaments, it is recommended that you prime the entire project with one of the following stain blocking primers: KILZ2, KILZ TOTAL ONE, H$_2$OIL BASE or Bulls Eye 1•2•3. If you are using pine or fir boards with *no* knots or defects which could bleed through the finish, a stain blocking primer is not necessary. You can use a regular exterior acrylic latex primer.

Spot Priming

The advantage of a stain blocking primer is its ability to prevent bleed through. If, for example, knots in the back of your plywood are the only area of concern, it would be entirely satisfactory to paint only those knots with a stain blocking primer. This is called "spot priming". After the potentially troublesome areas have been spot primed a regular exterior primer can be used to finished the job.

Acrylic Latex Primers

Acrylic latex primers are preferred for lawn ornaments and gloss or semi-gloss acrylic latex exterior paint is recommended for the top coat. As mentioned, latex primers and latex paint are more resistant to UV radiation and are less likely to blister than oil-based primer and paints. This is not to say that oil-based primers cannot be used. Oil-based primers do have their own advantages. For example, they have better "hiding" capabilities, and therefore better coverage. They also have better adhesion to wood and therefore seal the surface better. After considerable experimenting, we have found (top quality) latex primer and paint to be the all around best choice for painting lawn ornaments. The chart below outlines some of the advantages of latex vs. oil paints and primers:

	Latex	Oil
Drying Time	1-4 hours	24-48 hours
Vehicle	Non-flammable, Minimal offensive odor	Flammable, Toxic, mineral based
Fumes	Minimal risk of inhalation	Toxic. If used indoors must be well ventilated
Liquid Used for Thinning	Water	Paint thinner or turpentine
Clean-up	Warm water and soap	Paint thinner or turpentine

This chart summarizes the advantages of
using acrylic latex paint as compared to oil paint.

Three popular brands of water based stain blocking primers.
All are recommended for lawn ornaments.

Two popular brands of stain blocking primers. The product on the left is an oil base primer that cleans up with soap and water. The product on the right is a shellac based primer that cleans up with alcohol. Use this shellac based primer only for spot priming on outdoor projects.

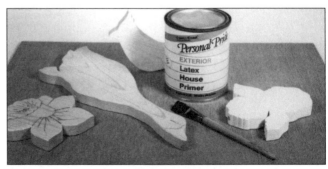
Most acrylic latex primers do not contain a stain blocking agent.
They can be used on wood which does not bleed excessive tannin
or contain knots or other defects which could bleed through.

More On Priming

Primer must be applied to bare wood prior to painting the top coat(s). Paint should not be used in place of primer. The reason is that primer contains less pigment. This allows it to better soak into the wood for a more adhesive grip. Primer is usually white. This is the preferred color for painting lawn ornaments in this book. (See Chapter 8.)

Tip: If you are making yard ornaments which are all the same color and have little interior detail, such as a 3-piece set of large bears or deer, try this: When you purchase your primer and paint, request that the primer be tinted the same color as the top coat. In this way, you will eliminate the problem of streaking, which sometimes occurs when you try to cover white primer with a single top coat of a dark color.

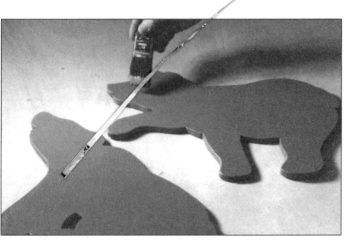

The primer was tinted to match the most dominant color of the top coat, therefore only one application of top coat was required on this set of brown bears.

Tip: Not all primers should be shaken on a paint shaker. Some manufacturers, such as Wm. Zinsser & Co., specify that their primers need little or no stirring, much less shaking. Zinsser sales personnel say that all shaking does is incorporate air, causing foam which must be dissipated before use or you will wind up with bubbles or craters. They recommend shaking their primers only when adding tint colors. Always read the manufacturer's label and follow their recommendations.

Avoid Heavy Coats

Don't apply extra heavy coats of either primer or paint. An extra heavy coat will not necessarily offer better protection. In fact, coats which are too thick will probably crack, resulting in less protection. While it is sometimes difficult to judge on a small object, try to use the coverage guidelines which the manufacturer has put on the label. If the label says that a gallon of paint will cover 400 square feet, and you have one hundred square feet of lawn ornaments to cover, then try to spread the paint so as to use up the quart over the 100 square feet of surface you are painting. This will result in the thickness of coating the manufacturer recommended.

Besides paint coverage, the label will advise the right drying time between coats. Always follow the label instructions. Manufacturers put a great deal of effort into research and development of their paint products. It is a good idea to get into the habit of reading and following label instructions.

Selecting the Paint for the Top Coats

You will want to select the best quality of paint available. It should also be compatible with the primer you have chosen. Look for exterior "trim" paint or "trim and shutter" paint. Trim paints are formulated for wood trim areas of the home. Other properties include good leveling (and therefore freedom from brush marks), rapid drying and good color retention. They are available in gloss or semi-gloss finishes, either of which are recommended for lawn ornaments.

When you purchase paints be sure to have your dealer shake them. This will help ensure that any pigment which may have sunk to the bottom of the can is resuspended. Also, be sure to ask the paint dealer for complimentary wood stir sticks. Use these wood sticks to mix the paint immediately upon opening the can to be absolutely sure the color is evenly distributed. Many hobbyists consider the painting of the final coat to be the most enjoyable part of making the project. Refer to Chapter 8 before applying the paint.

An example of an exterior latex paint suitable for "trim" work.

Always Read the Labels

Labels provide an amazing amount of information. Besides listing the directions for using the product, most manufacturers include safety information, storage and disposal hints. Below is a sample label. Look for the following information:

1. The Name of the Product.

2. Directions: The manufacturers go to a lot of work and expense to determine the best way for you to use their product. Be sure to read, understand and follow these directions.

3. Cautions: Read carefully to prevent any physical or health hazards.

4. The Manufacturer: The name, address, and emergency telephone number of the company that manufactured or imported the product.

5. Disposal: Used paint should be disposed of in an environmentally responsible manner.

An example of the type of information normally included on a paint label.

Choosing the Right Brush for the Job

Never skimp when it comes to the quality of paint brushes, especially for the finish coats. The use of quality brushes is the most important factor in getting a good paint job. Top quality brushes will not only help deliver a longer-lasting, better-looking paint job, but will save application time as well.

Quality paint and quality applicators are the least expensive part of a paint job. The labor involved in proper preparation and application is the most expensive part of the job.

Brushes are far and away the most popular application tool. They provide a smooth finish, are comfortable to hold, easy to clean, use the least amount of paint, and if cared for properly, will last a long time. Although not the most time-efficient tool to use, a quality paint brush is certainly the most versatile. There are two general types of paint brushes - those made of natural hair bristles and those made with synthetic materials (generally nylon or polyester).

For latex paint always choose a synthetic bristle brush. Natural bristle brushes tend to absorb water from the latex paint which causes the bristles to swell.

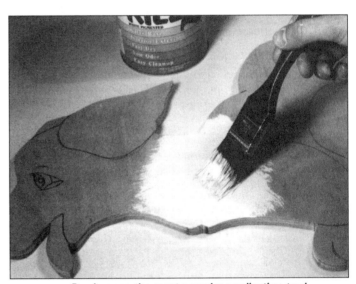

Brushes are the most popular application tool.

Quality Brush Characteristics

In choosing a quality paint brush, watch for these characteristics:

• The bristles should have split ends ("flags") that provide a finer, more even finish.

• The bristles should have a definite flex at their tips and easily spring back to shape.

• The bristles should be shorter on the outside and longer in the center, creating a tapered appearance. This type of "chiseled" brush gives the painter more control over where the paint will flow.

• The bristles should be at least half again as long as the width of the brush. For example, the bristles on a 2" wide brush should be 3" long.

• Tug on the bristles. If bristles can be pulled out, the brush is poorly constructed. A quality brush will shed only one or two bristles, at most.

For lawn ornaments, an assortment of artists brushes as well as 1-1/2" and 3" nylon bristle brushes are recommended. These brushes are pictured below.

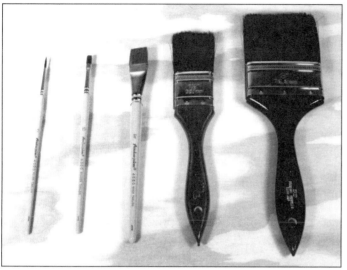

Recommended brushes for painting most lawn ornaments. Left to right: #3 Round, #6 Shader, 3/4" Flat Glaze artists brushes, 1-1/2"and 3" bristle brushes.

Like brushes, pads have the advantage of working the paint into the wood grain.

No Paint Rollers

Tip:

When using paint pads:
• Apply the paint with long, straight strokes.
• Never pull the pad back over the paint.
• Be aware that lap marks are more prone to occur with paint pads since the paint edges are difficult to feather with this tool.
• Use a roller tray when applying paint with a paint pad.

Paint Rollers

Paint rollers were specifically designed for painting interior walls. One advantage of painting with a roller is that a great deal of area can be covered rapidly and evenly.

But what about using rollers to apply paint to lawn ornaments? Perhaps to apply primer to both sides of several lawn ornaments? Would there be enough surface area to justify using a roller? Well, maybe, but even in this instance rollers are not recommended for lawn ornaments. Rollers should not be used over new wood because they do not allow paint to work into the wood grain! This is important because the primer and subsequent paint coatings must be applied in the correct way to get the longest life.

Paint Pads

In the example above where you are priming both sides of several lawn ornaments, a paint pad would be better than a roller. Like brushes, pads have the advantage of working the paint into the wood grain. (Always brush in the same direction as the grain.)

Cleaning Paint Brushes

Brushes should be cleaned immediately after you are finished painting. By using the following cleaning procedure, brushes will last a long time. Note: This cleaning procedure is for primers and paints formulated for clean-up with soap and water.

First, remove excess paint by pulling the bristles across the inside edge of the paint can several times, turning the brush after each pull.

Next, run warm water over the bristles, using your fingers to help work out the paint.

Then, rub bristles with a liquid detergent such as Pine-Sol®, Tide® or Palmolive®. Work the detergent into the bristles with your fingers.

Lastly, rinse the brush in warm water until no more paint can be seen dissolving into the water.

Wrap the brushes in a paper towel and let dry.

CHAPTER 8

Priming & Painting

Before Applying the Primer

Before applying the primer, be sure the following steps have been taken:

1. All interior lines have been transferred to the wood with carbon paper.

2. These interior lines have been re-traced with a blue ball point pen.

These two steps are important for the painting of the top coat. The ink from the blue ball point pen will bleed through one or two coats of primer (even stain blocking primer). This bleed through is desirable because it will identify the location of the interior lines. This makes a convenient guide for the various colors of the top coat and eliminates the danger of smudges which could result if carbon paper was used on top of the primer coats. Although the ink from the ball point pen has an amazing ability to bleed through the primer, if two coats of primer are being used, it may be necessary to retrace the interior lines before the application of the second coat. Test a small area to check for the amount of bleed-through before painting each coat. Note: It takes about 10 to 20 minutes for the ink to show through after the primer has been applied.

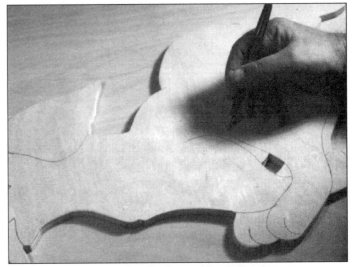

Trace over the interior lines with a ball point pen.

Don't forget the back of the plywood. If you will be detailing the back of your project, use a blue ball point pen to retrace the necessary interior lines before priming. If you have made a polyethylene pattern simply turn it over, and use carbon paper to transfer the paint lines. Remove the poly pattern and carbon paper, and go back over the interior lines with a ball point pen.

In the photos on the following page, interior lines are being transferred to the back of the wood, (with a poly pattern) and the interior lines are being re-traced with a blue ball point pen.

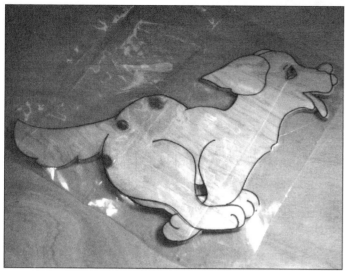

Turn the project and poly pattern over.

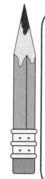*Tip:* For extraordinarily smooth edges, apply waterproof glue to the edges of the plywood. Use your finger to work Titebond II® Water Resistant Glue all around the edge of the plywood. This glue is very paintable and so the primer coats will adhere to it. With light sanding, this method leaves a very smooth surface which will enhance the appearance of the finished lawn ornament.

Applying the Primer

Sap streaks and knots are normally found on the back of A-C grade plywood. They may bleed through the paint if the correct primer is not used. Choose a stain blocking primer to spot prime these troublesome areas. Then prime the entire project with a quality acrylic latex primer. Or prime the entire project with a stain blocking primer followed by exterior acrylic latex paint for the top coat(s).

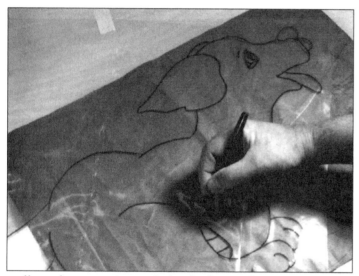

Use carbon paper to transfer interior lines to the back of the plywood.

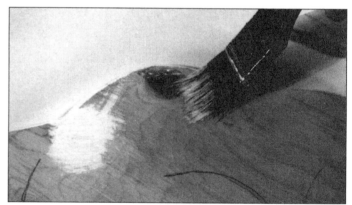

Spot prime sap streaks or knots with stain-blocking primer to prevent bleed through.

Use a two to three inch nylon brush to prime the unpainted wood. Don't forget to prime all surfaces of the project. The edges are the most vulnerable to moisture. Follow the directions on the label. The manufacturer may have specific guidelines for mixing and application. When applying the primer, always brush in the same direction as the grain for better penetration into the wood. After the first coat of primer, the grain of the wood may raise, causing a rough surface. Sanding between primer coats will make it smooth and paintable.

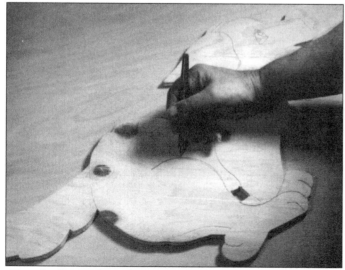

Trace back over the carbon paper lines with a blue ball point pen.

Sanding the Primer

Sanding the primer will provide a smooth surface for the top coats. A second coat of primer is recommended by some, but not all manufacturers. Two coats of primer are recommended on the *edges* of plywood.

Sanding can be accomplished by hand or by machine. If hand sanding, wrap a piece of 100 grit sandpaper around a block of wood and sand *with* the direction of the grain. Sand the edges by holding the sandpaper with your fingers. Pad sanders and palm sanders can be used for sanding the front and back of the plywood. They make the job go much faster. Power sanders should be fitted with 100 grit sandpaper.

Example of a palm sander.

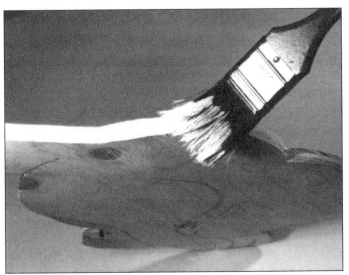

The edges are important when priming and painting.

Painting the Project

Once the project has been cut, prepared and primed, it's time for the really fun part! The painting of your project can be very satisfying. Many people say that when they are painting their projects, they feel a great sense of accomplishment. The plans provided in this book provide color suggestions. Feel free to select other colors if you desire. Exterior acrylic latex paint in either gloss or semi-gloss finish is recommended for the top coats.

Amount of Paint to Purchase

Color selection, of course, depends on which projects you decide to make. If only the Running Geese are being made, then only white and yellow paint will be needed. If you plan to make a variety of lawn ornaments, the following assortment can be considered as a "starting set". By mixing various amounts of white, blue, red, yellow, brown and black paints, all of the colors in the mixing chart on page 48 can be created. To get started begin by purchasing the following:

White	1 Quart
Blue	1 Pint
Red	1 Pint
Yellow	1 Pint
Black	1 Pint
Medium Brown	1 Pint

Depending on the number of projects you will be making and the amount of each color required, pint size or half-pint size cans of paint may be adequate. Naturally, if painting a lot of one color it is most economical to purchase larger size cans of those colors. Colors can be used straight or they can be mixed to create all colors needed for the projects in this book.

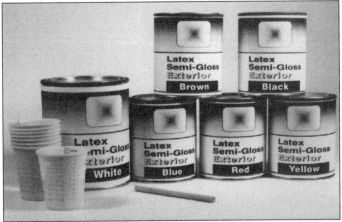

Examples of exterior latex paint, portion cups and a dowel for stirring.

Tip: Start with the lightest color and continue to the next darker color. In this way, the darker color will cover the lighter color in case of accidental overlap. Black is painted last. In most patterns you have a fair amount of freedom when painting the features. The spots on the dogs, for example, can be placed just about anywhere.

Multiple Yard Ornaments

When painting many projects at once, try to paint all of the same colors one after another. For example, if the Running Dog is white with brown spots, paint the edges and one side of the dog white. Next proceed to the Running Geese, the apron of the Little Farmer Girl, and any other areas that are white. Now, go back to the first project and if the paint has sufficiently dried, turn it over and paint the back. Continue until all the white areas on the projects are done. Then select the next darker color and paint where required.

Example of a painting jig to be used on projects made from 3/4" stock. (These projects have a 1/4" hole for the fiberglass mounting dowel.) This jig is made from scrap wood and 1/4" wood dowels.

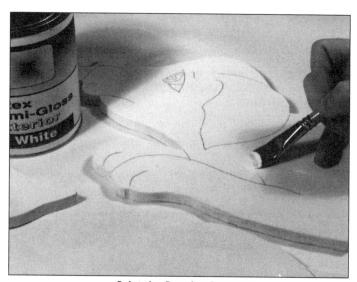

Paint the Running Dog white.

Yard Flowers, Yard Birds, Running Geese or any smaller project made from 3/4" stock can be held in a painting jig. This allows you to get at all sides of the project. A dowel mounted to a scrap wood base makes a convenient painting jig. Drill a 1/4" hole in the bottom of the project. This hole will be used again for the fiberglass mounting dowel.

Painting jigs allow you to paint all sides of the project.

Mixing Colors

Almost any color can be created by mixing basic colors. To make flesh for the hands and face of the Climbing Boy and Little Farmer Girl, start with 1-1/2 oz. of white paint in a portion cup or other container. Portion cups are preferred because they are marked in ounces, teaspoons and milliliter graduations. Next add 3/4 oz. of yellow and 1/8 oz. of red. Finish by lowering a 1/4" dowel (a popsicle stick or sawed off pencil will also work well) into a can of blue paint to a depth of one inch. This will give about the right amount of blue tint. Use the dowel to stir the mixture thoroughly. This will produce a good flesh color. Consult the paint chart for mixing other colors. The markings on the sides of the portion cups make it easy to measure the correct amount of paint.

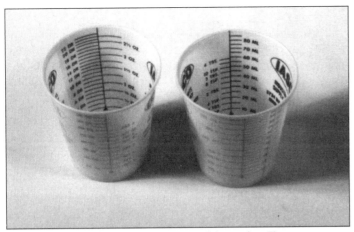

Portion cups are useful when mixing paint. They are graduated in ounces, teaspoons and milliliters. Available by mail from Meisel Hardware Specialties.

Here's how to use portion cups to mix flesh colored paint. All paint proportions are shown in the Paint Mixing Chart on page 48.

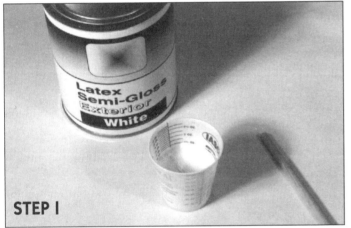

STEP 1

To mix flesh colored paint begin with 1-1/2 ounces of white in a portion cup.

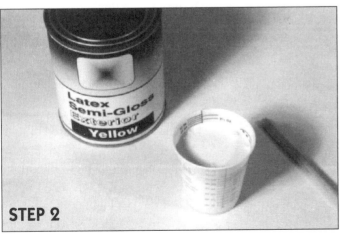

STEP 2

Add 3/4 oz. of yellow paint.

STEP 3

Add 1/8 oz. red.

STEP 4

Lower a 1/4" dowel (or pencil) into a can of blue paint to a depth of one inch. Using this dowel, mix thoroughly to get a flesh color.

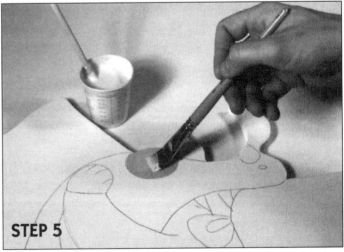

STEP 5

Paint the hands flesh with a 3/4" Flat Glaze brush. Remember to paint any other projects which require flesh tone at this time.

Paint Mixing Chart

This chart shows the mixture of various paint colors, in ounces, recommended for the projects in this book. Use this mixing chart only as a general guide. Colors will vary depending on the tint of the paint you are mixing. These colors were created by using basic primary colors.

Note: The batch sizes for pink and gray are slightly larger (6oz.) than the other colors. This is to accommodate the Pink Flamingos and gray Squirrels. Helpful hint: Two teaspoons equal about 1/4 oz.

COLOR	FLESH	ORANGE	GREEN	PINK	LIGHT BLUE	PURPLE	LIGHT PURPLE	DARK YELLOW	LIGHT YELLOW	BROWN**	LIGHT BROWN	GRAY	DARK RED**
White	1-1/2			4	3	1/4	1/2		3/4			4	
Blue	Trace*		3/4		1	3/8	3/8			1/8	1/8		
Red	1/8	5/8		2		1/2	1/2	3/16		1	3/4		1-1/2
Yellow	3/4	1-1/2	1-1/2					1-3/4	1/4	1	1-1/2		
Black		1/16.						1/16		1/2	1/4	2	
Brown**													1/2
BATCH AMOUNT	2- 3/8 oz.	2-3/16 oz.	2-1/4 oz.	6 oz.	4 oz.	1-1/8oz.	1-3/8 oz.	2 oz.	1 oz.	2-5/8 oz.	2-5/8 oz.	6 oz.	2 oz.

*Only a trace amount of blue paint is needed. Suggestion: Dip a 1/4" dowel to the depth of 1" in the paint can, then use that dowel to mix paint.

**You may purchase brown paint or you can make your own following the paint chart. When making dark red, use either the purchased paint or your own mixture.

Application Techniques

These techniques will help ensure your painting job looks as good as possible.

Before starting, clear the brush of loose bristles by striking the flat side of the brush sharply across the heel of your hand several times. In this operation, most loose bristles will fly out. Those that don't come out completely will protrude at the brush end and can be easily removed.

Try moistening the brush with water before applying latex paint. Slightly damp brushes will apply the paint more evenly. Do not overload the brush with paint. Dip only one-third to one-half the length of the bristles into the paint can, then tap - not wipe - the brush against the side of the can. Brush at about a 45 degree angle to the surface. The paint should be applied in long, light strokes. Follow the direction of grain whenever possible.

To avoid lap marks, always brush toward the unpainted area and then back into the just-painted surface. This technique (brushing from "wet to dry", rather than vice versa) will produce a smooth, uniform appearance.

While some extra brushing may improve the appearance of oil-based paints, excessive rebrushing should be avoided when using water-based or latex paints, especially semi-gloss or gloss finishes. To achieve a thick paint film with good hiding, just a few strokes will suffice with latex paints.

Clean the Brush Before the Next Color

To prepare the brush for the next color, first brush out excess paint on a newspaper, then rinse the brush with warm water. When it no longer gives off paint, "towel dry" with a paper towel and proceed with the next darker color.

After you have finished painting for the day, thoroughly clean all brushes. See Chapter 7 for more suggestions on brush cleaning.

Using Paint Markers

After all colors of the top coat have been painted, it is time to add highlights with a paint marker. Paint markers are similar to felt tip markers, except they contain real paint rather than ink. (Felt pens, even those with permanent ink, are not recommended because the ink will sunfade within a few weeks.) Use the black paint marker to go all around the perimeter of the project. Next, highlight the area where each color meets. This gives a remarkable clarity to the finished project.

Paint markers come in different sizes. The medium line is satisfactory for all the projects in this book. Fine lines are not easily seen from a distance and are used less frequently. Use a medium line when tracing the perimeter, as well as most interior lines such as legs, arms, etc. A fine line paint marker can be used for fine details, such as the eyes on the Dogs.

Shown here are medium and fine line paint markers.
Caution: Paint markers emit a strong odor. Use in well ventilated area. When weather permits, it is best to use them outdoors.

Tip: When tracing the perimeter with the paint marker, take advantage of the edge. The edge will help maintain some control, in effect giving you a uniform line.

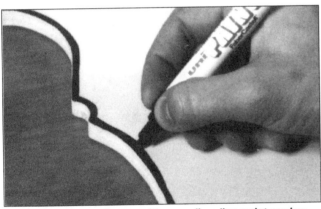

First trace the perimeter with a medium line paint marker.

Then use a medium line and a fine line paint marker to highlight interior lines.

CHAPTER 9

Displaying Your Lawn Ornaments

There are various ways to mount lawn ornaments. For the smaller ornaments that are cut from 3/4" boards, it is easiest to drill a 1/4" hole in the bottom and add a fiberglass rod. The fiberglass rod can be glued in place if desired. Wood dowels are not recommended because they simply do not hold up well outdoors. Most wood dowels are made from birch. Birch rots faster than many other wood species. In addition, wood dowels absorb moisture and easily snap off when subject to a sudden gust of high wind or a stray basketball which might roll out into the yard.

A 9 inch fiberglass rod makes it easy to remove and reposition the Running Geese as shown in Chapter 2. When displayed in the lawn, the geese will likely be viewed from both sides. By mounting the rod in the bottom, both sides of the project will be unobstructed.

For the Yard Bird below, a three inch fiberglass rod is used for the mounting stake. A 1/4" hole is drilled in the bottom of the bird and another hole is drilled where the bird will be displayed. These Yard Birds are typically mounted on a fence, building, or a tree trunk or branch.

The 1/4" fiberglass rods used for these Yard Flower stems are unbreakable. They are also paintable.

For projects made from 1/2" plywood, it is best to mount fiberglass dowels to the back of the project with metal brackets. For larger projects, use 3/8" fiberglass rods. For smaller projects, 1/4" fiberglass rods are satisfactory. These rods can be painted, if desired.

Tip: Before attaching the fiberglass rod, use a disc sander to sand a sharp point. This will make it easier to push the finished project into the ground.

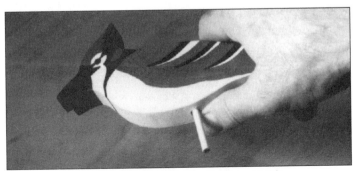

A hole was drilled in the bottom of this Yard Bird and then a fiberglass dowel was inserted.

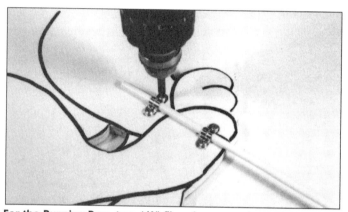

This 30" high lawn ornament is mounted with 3/8" x 18" long fiberglass dowels. They are attached to the back of the project with metal brackets.

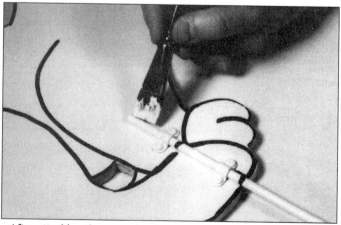

For the Running Dog, two 1/4" fiberglass mounting rods are sufficient. They are attached to the back with metal brackets.

Since the backside of the Running Dog is visible, the fiberglass rods and the mounting brackets were painted to make them blend in.

Mounting Kits

Lawn ornament mounting kits are available via mail order from Meisel Hardware Specialties. These kits include two fiberglass rods, four metal strap brackets and attachment screws.

Lawn ornament mounting kits are available in two sizes, 1/4" and 3/8".

Wood stakes can also be used to mount lawn ornaments. The major disadvantage is that they cannot be easily removed from the lawn. This adds trimming time when mowing the lawn.

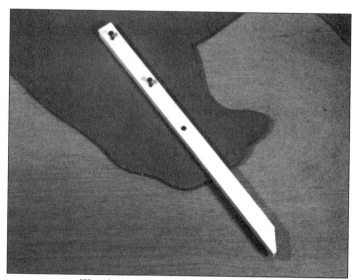

Wood mounting stakes can be used, but are far more difficult to push into the lawn.

After attaching the mounting brackets and stakes, touch up with paint.

Frozen Ground or Hard Surfaces

Decorating with lawn ornaments in the winter, when the ground is frozen, adds a new challenge. Stakes typically cannot be pushed into the frozen ground. The solution is to drill a hole into the ground the diameter of the mounting rod. This makes the insertion of the rod into the ground almost effortless.

If a cement patio is the location you wish to decorate, mounting rods simply may not be practical. In this case, try making wood brackets suitable to hold a cement block or other weight.

Hanger brackets are used for attaching projects to houses, trees, fences, etc.

A cement block provides the weight to keep this snowman upright. The sides and the bottom are attached with screws so they can be removed for storage.

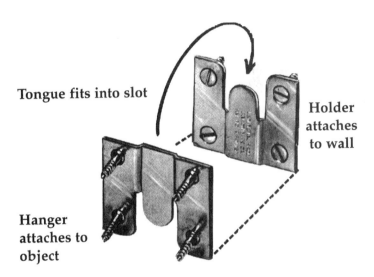

Tongue fits into slot

Holder attaches to wall

Hanger attaches to object

Diagram of Bracket

Hanger Brackets

Hanger brackets work well for attaching lawn ornaments to a tree, fence or building. These brackets consist of interlocking pieces. Attach one side to the project and the other side to the surface you will be decorating. Two hanger bracket sets are recommended for each lawn ornament. By mounting these brackets the same distance apart on all lawn ornaments, it is easy to switch from one ornament to another as the seasons change. The brackets are available via mail order from Meisel Hardware Specialties (Part #1262).

Tip: Some lawn ornaments are particularly good candidates for mounting with brackets. The Boy Climbing is a good example. He can be replaced by a ghost or flying witch at Halloween, then an angel or Santa during Christmas.

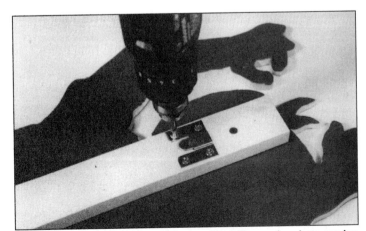

Attaching the bracket to the lawn ornament. Hanger brackets can be mounted directly to the back of the project. If the tree has an irregular shape, wood spacers may be required for additional clearance.

Attach one 3/4" wood strip with brackets to a tree and another to the back of your lawn ornament.

Boy Climbing a tree.

Changing for the Sake of Change

Just as different flowers bloom in the spring than in the fall, so can different lawn ornaments be displayed for different seasons. You may simply switch the arrangement of your yard grouping, or choose to replace them with a completely different grouping. Lawn ornaments lend themselves to seasonal decorating. Patterns are available for Easter, St. Patrick's Day, Fourth of July, Halloween, Thanksgiving and Christmas from Meisel Hardware Specialties. Brand new designs are being created each season. If there are additional designs you would like to request, write to me- Paul Meisel. I appreciate all suggestions and would be happy to hear from any reader. I hope you will send pictures of your yard. I will include as many reader photos as I can in the next edition of this book.

Hanger brackets make it easy to switch to this ghost for Halloween.

Maintenance

Maintenance? You mean lawn ornaments don't last forever? Anytime painted wood projects are exposed to the harsh outdoor environment, there will be some deterioration. Even paint which is especially developed for exterior use will eventually fade and peel.

Yard ornaments are not "forever". At a minimum, expect them to last two to five years - more if they are located in an area protected from rain and direct sun, less if you live in a hot and humid climate.

But then, that's OK. After all, the charm is changing them periodically. And part of the fun is making them in the first place. So don't be afraid to periodically repaint your projects or even make new ones. You did buy this book because you are a hobbyist woodworker, right?

Warping

Warping is a problem which sometimes occurs. This large bear warped when exposed to the elements for only a few weeks. Of the hundreds of lawn ornaments we have made, we only rarely experience warping.

Or display a flying witch.

Switch to an Angel or Santa for Christmas.

Large Bear lawn ornament that warped when exposed to the elements.

Bracing may be used to lend support to plywood, however it is not always practical for lawn ornaments, especially if they are to be viewed from both sides. No matter how carefully you prepare plywood, conditions beyond your control could cause it to warp. In these rare cases it may be best to simply scrap the project and make another one. In the case of the bear ornament (above), it was decided to display it in the yard despite the warp. Even after an entire season, no one seemed to notice the warp.

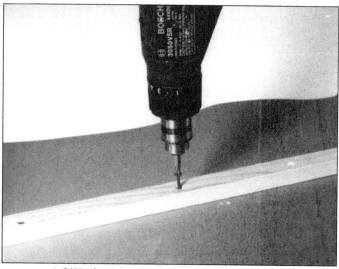

A 3/4" pine brace can be used to give added support to help prevent warping of lawn ornaments.

Storing Lawn Ornaments

There are various reasons for putting lawn ornaments in temporary storage. Seasonal ornaments, such as those for Halloween or Christmas, are displayed only during their respective seasons. Many people in northern climates put their lawn ornaments away during the winter. A boy in a short-sleeved shirt looks somewhat out of place during a cold Minnesota winter. And in areas where deep winter snowfalls would bury the lawn ornaments, it makes no sense to leave the projects out.

Care must be taken to prevent accidental damage to projects while they are not being used. A simple storage rack can be hung from the garage rafters to stack lawn ornaments. This keeps them safe and completely out of the way. It is a good idea to wrap the yard ornaments in polyethylene to protect them from getting scratched and to keep them clean.

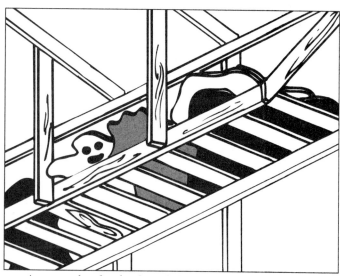

An example of a simple rack for storing yard ornaments.

About the pattern section...

Directions and suggestions for transferring the patterns to your wood are given in Chapter 4. The two preferred methods are:

1) Photocopying the pattern. For multiple page patterns trim off the border and tape the adjoining pages together.

2) Making a poly pattern.

As an alternative, please note that the pattern pages can be removed from the book and, by using carbon paper, transferred directly to your wood. The patterns have been positioned on the pages with this in mind. For example, the Running Dog requires four pages of the book (Pages 82, 83, 86 and 87.) Once these pages have been removed, trimmed to size, and taped together, it will be seen upon turning the assembly over that the Standing Dog (Pages 81, 84, 85 and 88.) will appear in the correct order on the other side. Note that the tail for Robby Raccoon is fastened to the body with a wood screw. The illustration on the pattern shows three different ways to position the tail on the body. The Uncle Sam pattern is on five separate pages. Uncle Sam has a hand that connects to the area shown by the "match line" on page 119. The pattern for the hand is on page 121. When the project is displayed, the hand makes a good place to attach a small American flag. The Scarecrow makes an excellent yard decoration for the Fall of the year or it can be used to decorate the garden.

Note also that each pattern contains a suggested material either 1/2" plywood or 3/4" softwood boards. (The flamingos can be made from either 3/4" boards or 3/4" plywood.) All patterns which are cut from 1/2" plywood should be mounted by the method of attaching fiberglass stakes to the back with metal brackets and 1/2" sheet metal screws. All projects made from 3/4" thick stock should be drilled with 1/4" holes and mounted with 1/4" fiberglass dowels. For the Yard Critters, a single fiberglass rod extends from the flag through the body, and into the ground. The flag should say HI on one side and BYE on the other. (On the yard flamingos, use 3/8" holes and 3/8" dowels for mounting.)

List of Patterns...

Description	Page
Rabbits	59, 60
Barnyard Chickens	61, 64, 65, 68
Yard Flamingos	62, 63, 66, 67
Running Geese	69, 72
Climbing Boy	70, 71, 74, 75, 78, 79
Feeding Squirrel	73, 76
Calico Hen and Chicks	77, 80
Standing Dog	81, 84, 85, 88
Running Dog	82, 83, 86, 87
Climbing Dog	89, 92, 93, 96
Sniffing Dog	90, 91, 94, 95
Yard Flowers	97, 100, 102
Little Farmer Girl	98, 99, 101
Yard Geese	103, 104, 105, 106
Yard Birds	114, 128
Robby Raccoon	107, 110, 111
Running Cat	108, 109
Running Squirrel	112, 113
Uncle Sam	115, 117, 119, 121, 123
Scarecrow	116, 118, 125, 127
Hi/Bye Critters	120, 122, 124, 126

RABBITS
CUT FROM 1/2" EXTERIOR PLYWOOD

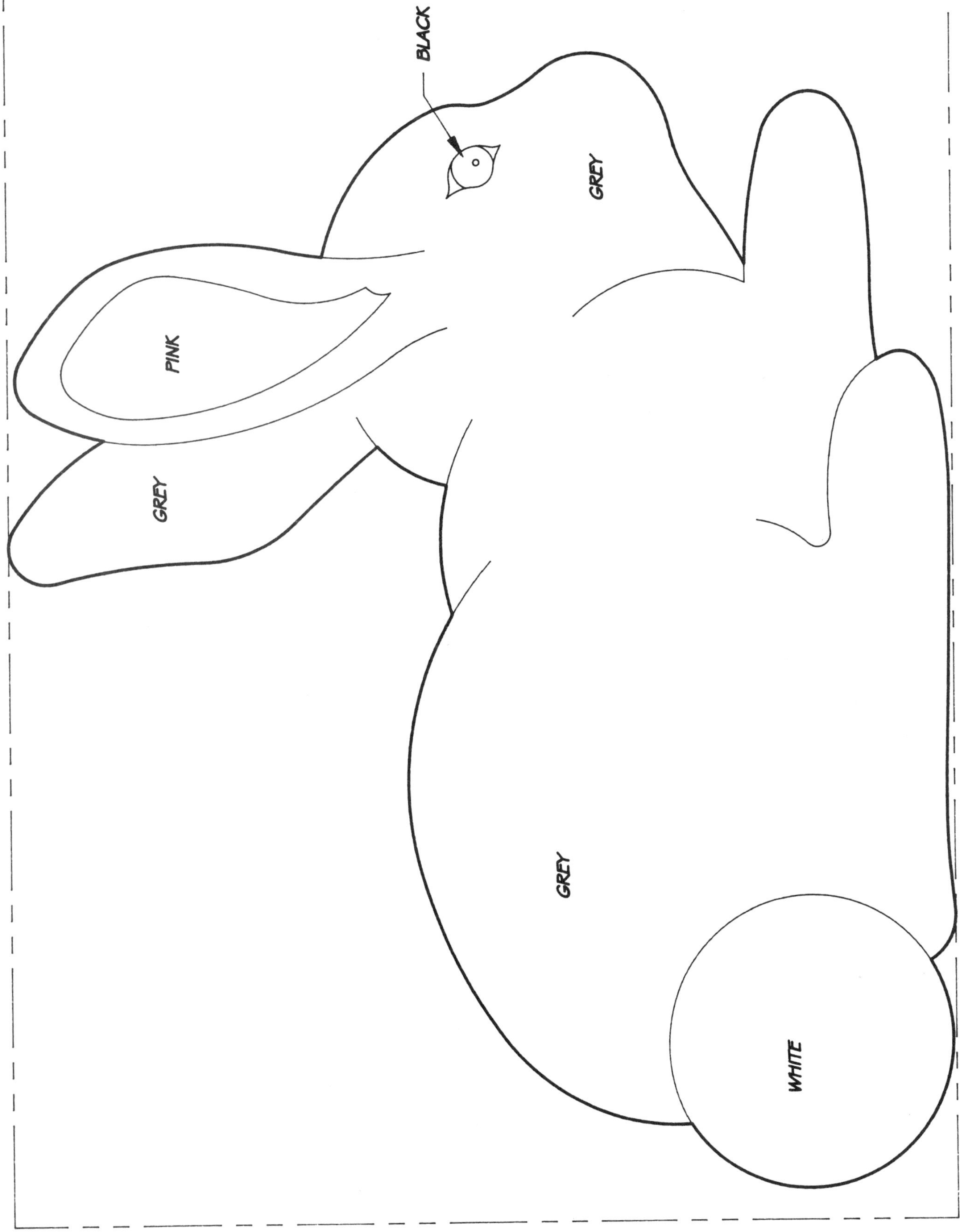

BLACK

GREY

PINK

GREY

GREY

WHITE

RABBITS
CUT FROM 1/2" EXTERIOR PLYWOOD

BLACK

WHITE

WHITE

WHITE

WHITE

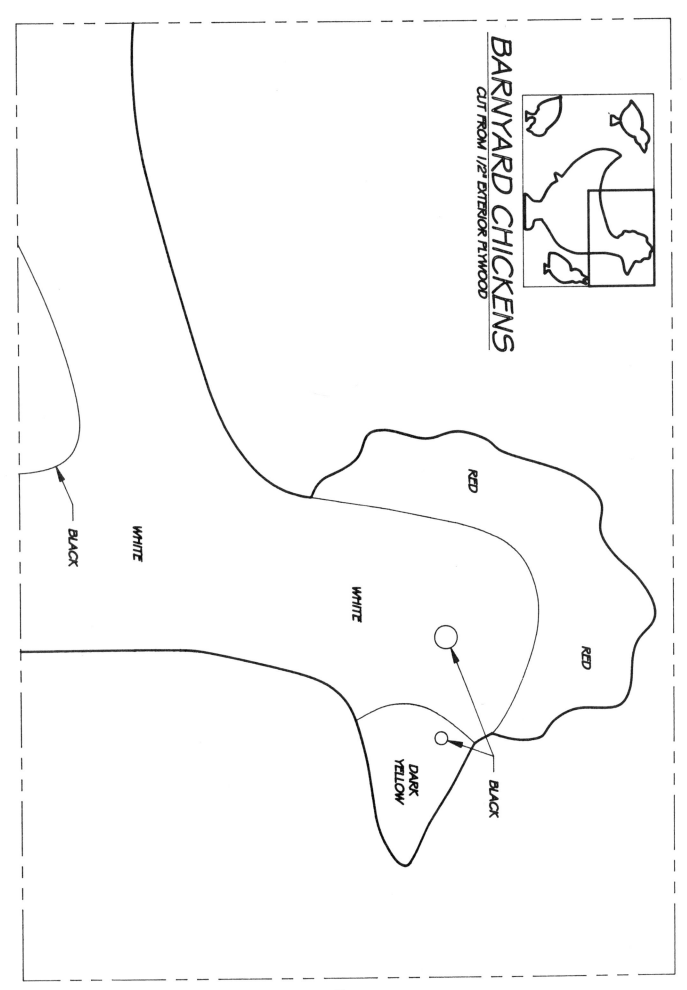

BARNYARD CHICKENS
CUT FROM 1/2" EXTERIOR PLYWOOD

RED

WHITE

WHITE

RED

BLACK

BLACK

DARK
YELLOW

BLACK

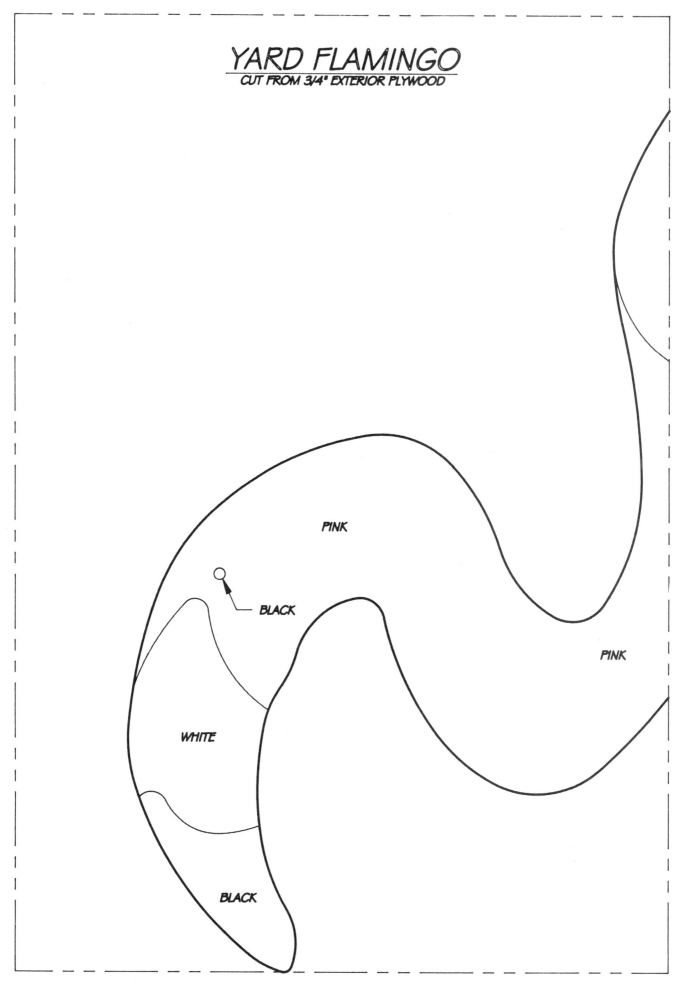

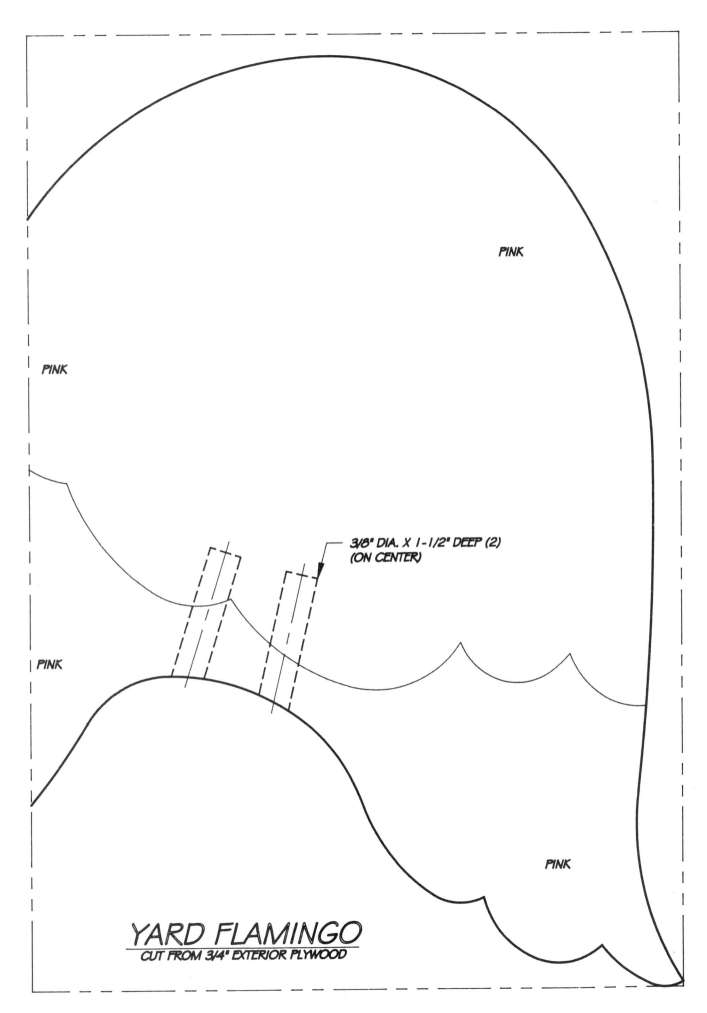

PINK

PINK

3/8" DIA. X 1-1/2" DEEP (2)
(ON CENTER)

PINK

YARD FLAMINGO
CUT FROM 3/4" EXTERIOR PLYWOOD

PINK

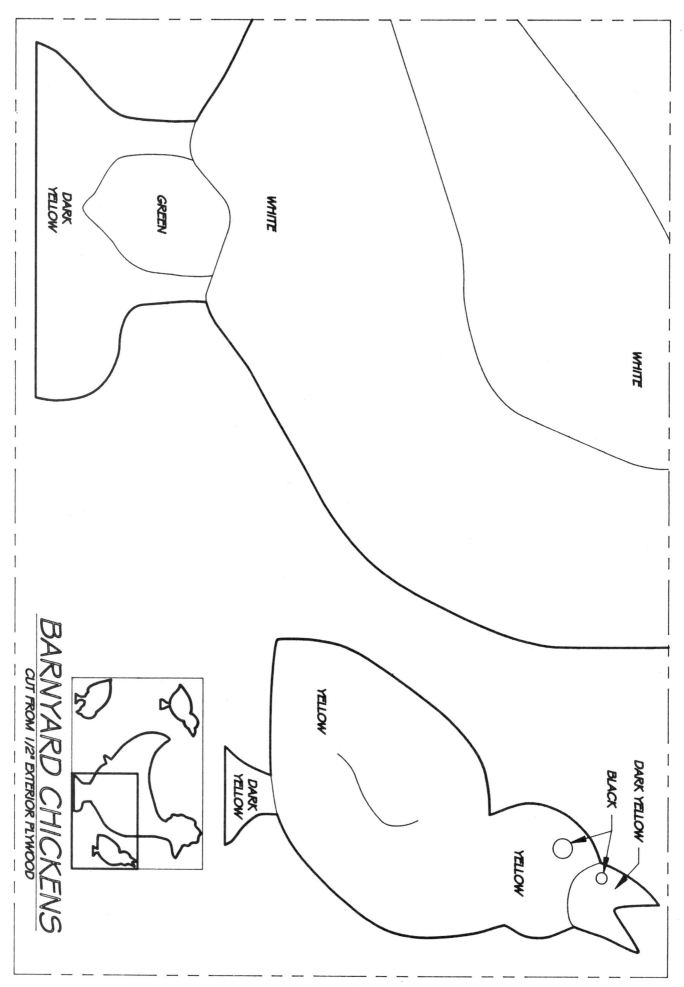

DARK YELLOW

GREEN

WHITE

WHITE

YELLOW

DARK YELLOW

DARK YELLOW

BLACK

YELLOW

BARNYARD CHICKENS
CUT FROM 1/2" EXTERIOR PLYWOOD

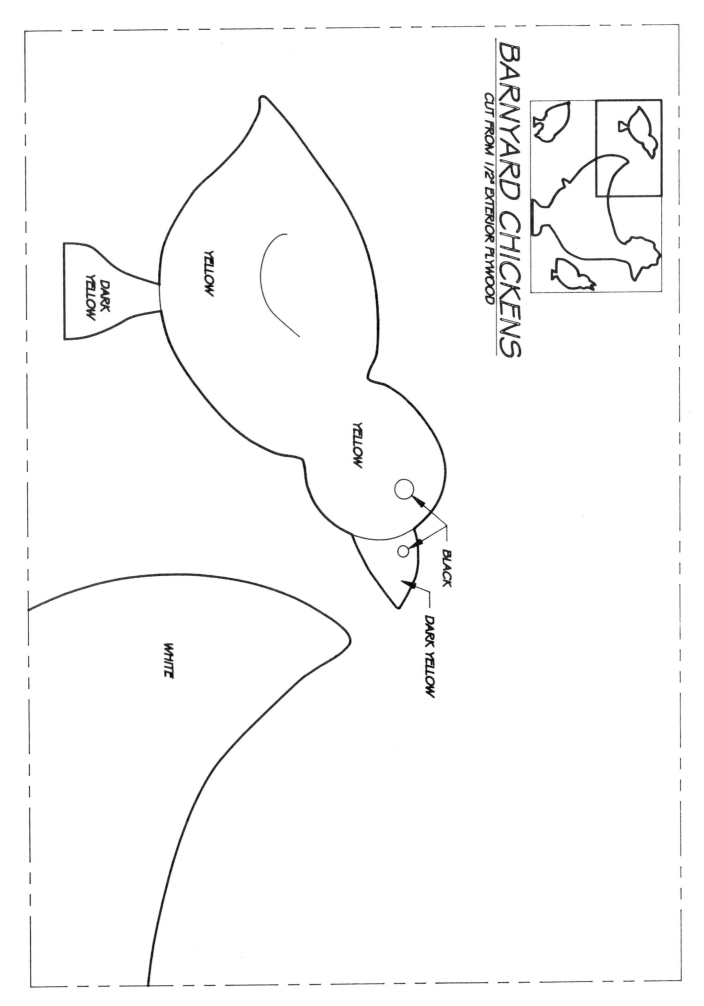

BARNYARD CHICKENS
CUT FROM 1/2" EXTERIOR PLYWOOD

YELLOW

DARK
YELLOW

YELLOW

BLACK

DARK YELLOW

WHITE

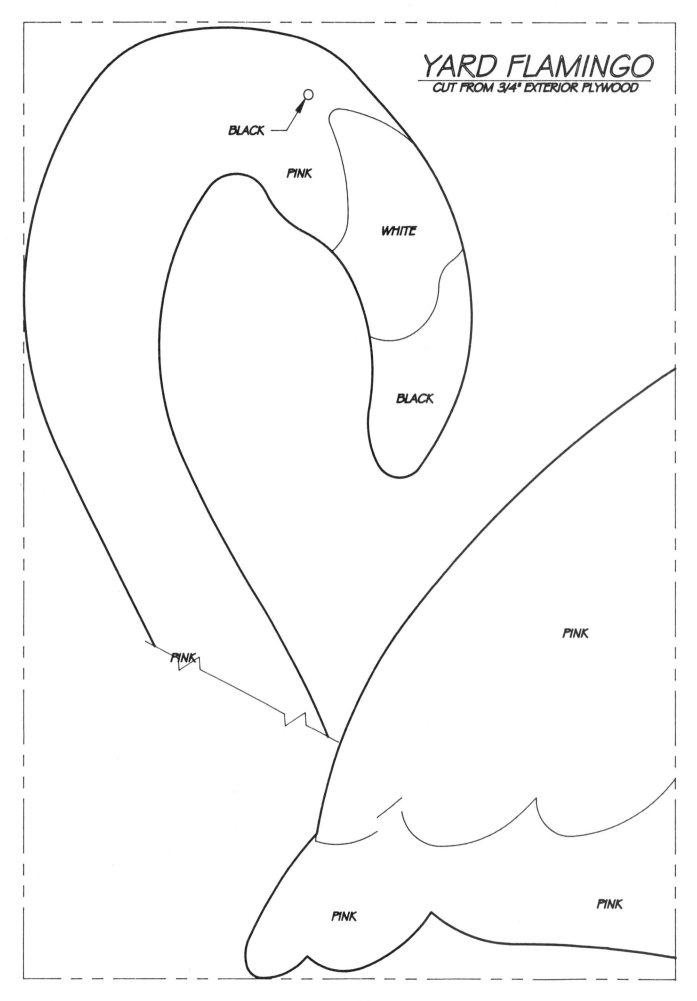

YARD FLAMINGO
CUT FROM 3/4" EXTERIOR PLYWOOD

BLACK

PINK

WHITE

BLACK

PINK

PINK

PINK

PINK

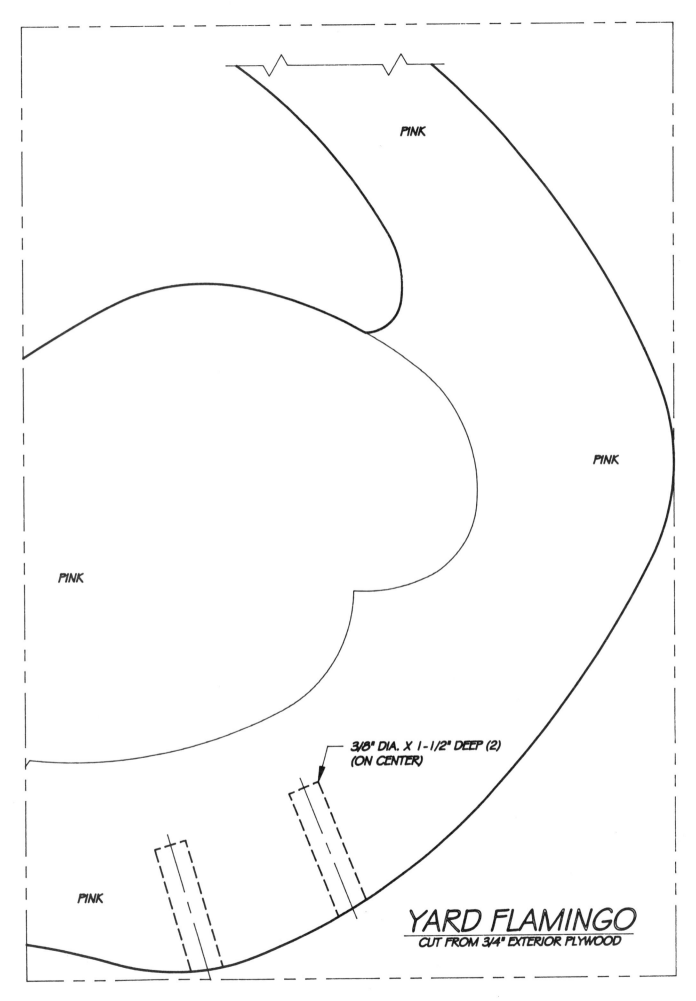

PINK

PINK

PINK

3/8" DIA. X I-1/2" DEEP (2)
(ON CENTER)

PINK

YARD FLAMINGO
CUT FROM 3/4" EXTERIOR PLYWOOD

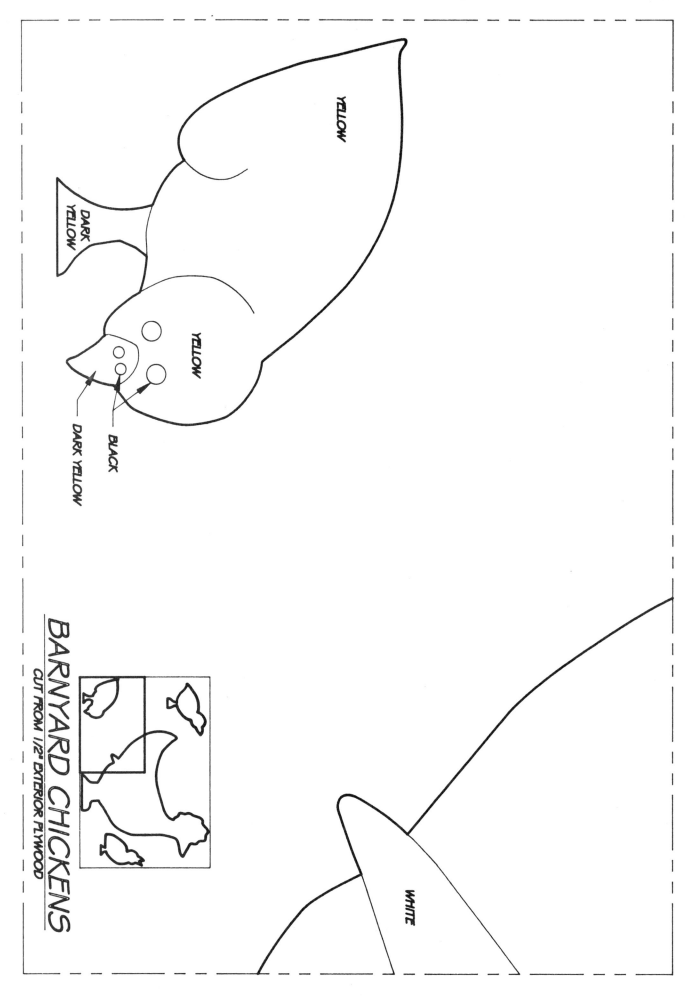

YELLOW

DARK
YELLOW

YELLOW

DARK YELLOW

BLACK

BARNYARD CHICKENS
CUT FROM 1/2" EXTERIOR PLYWOOD

WHITE

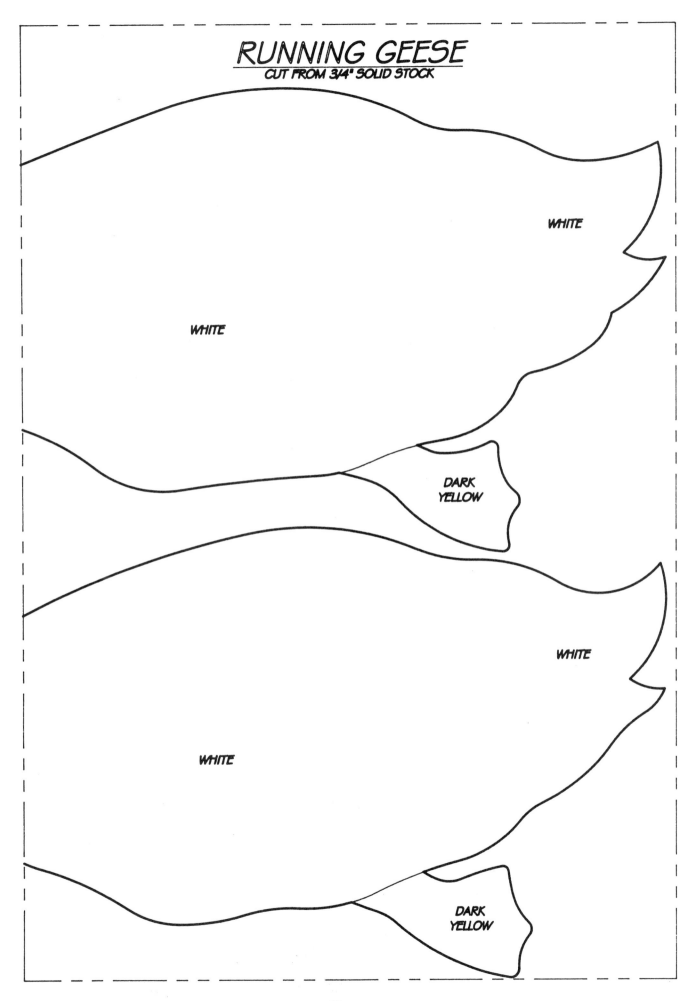

RUNNING GEESE
CUT FROM 3/4" SOLID STOCK

WHITE

WHITE

DARK YELLOW

WHITE

WHITE

DARK YELLOW

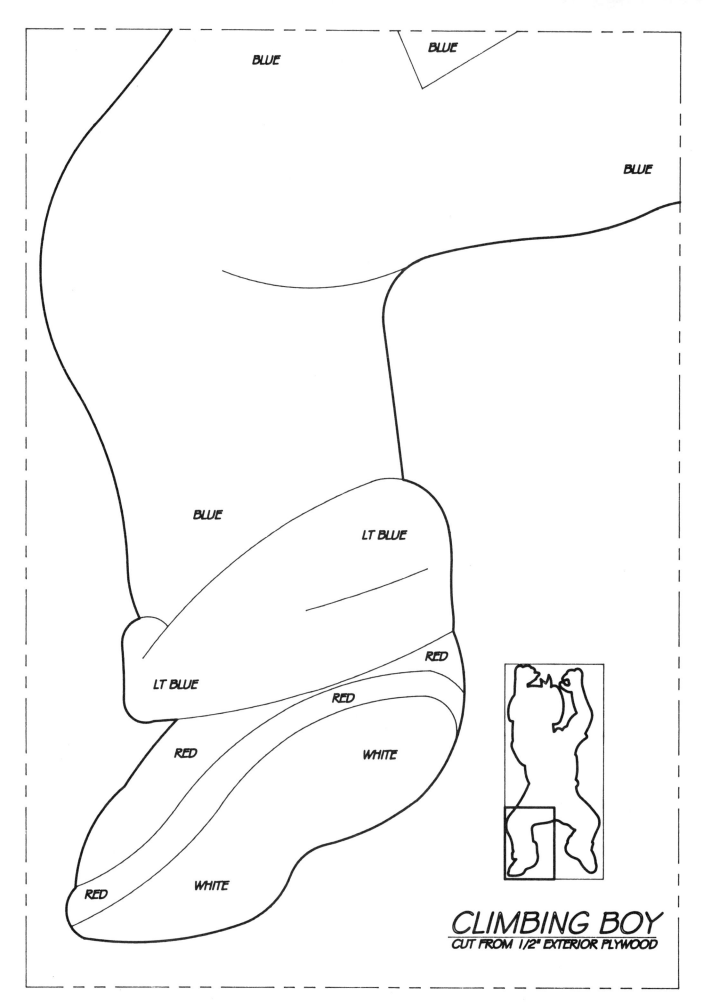

BLUE

BLUE

BLUE

BLUE

LT BLUE

RED

LT BLUE

RED

RED

WHITE

RED

WHITE

RED

CLIMBING BOY
CUT FROM 1/2" EXTERIOR PLYWOOD

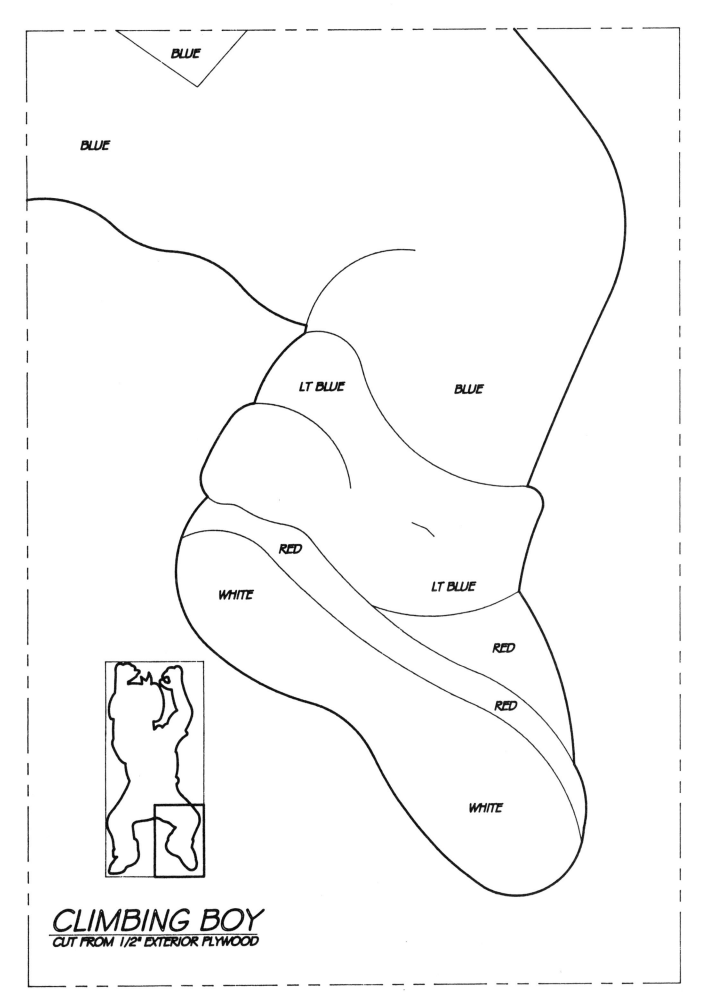

CLIMBING BOY
CUT FROM 1/2" EXTERIOR PLYWOOD

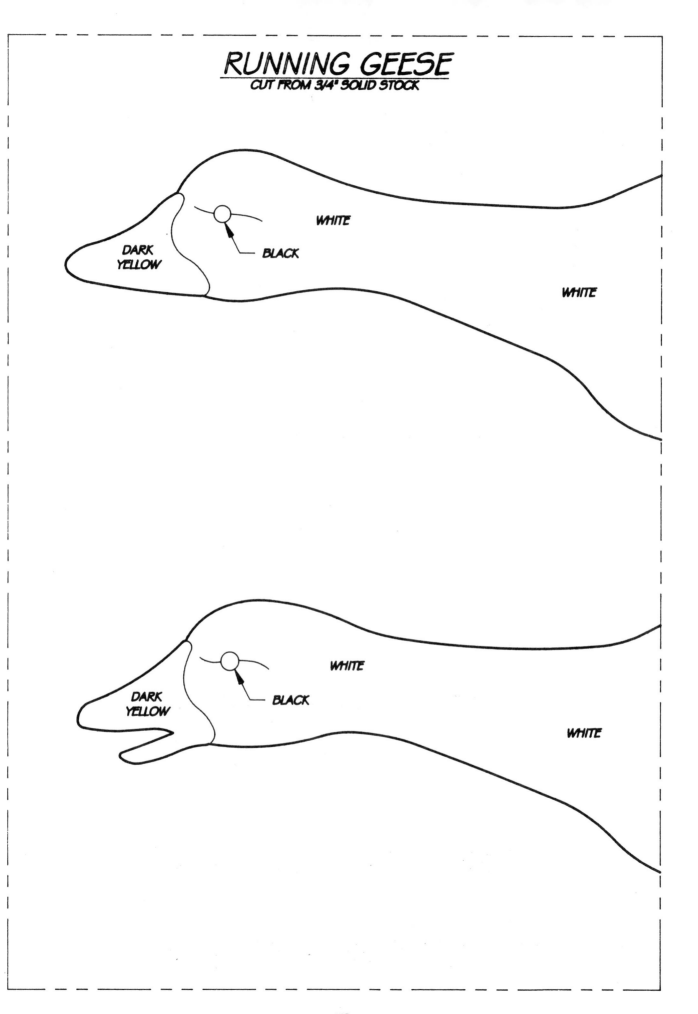

FEEDING SQUIRREL
CUT FROM 1/2" EXTERIOR PLYWOOD

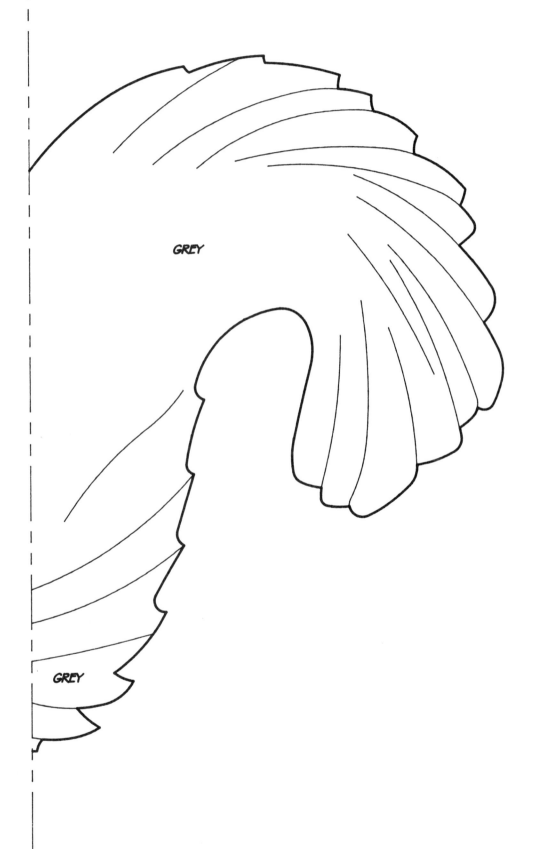

GREY

GREY

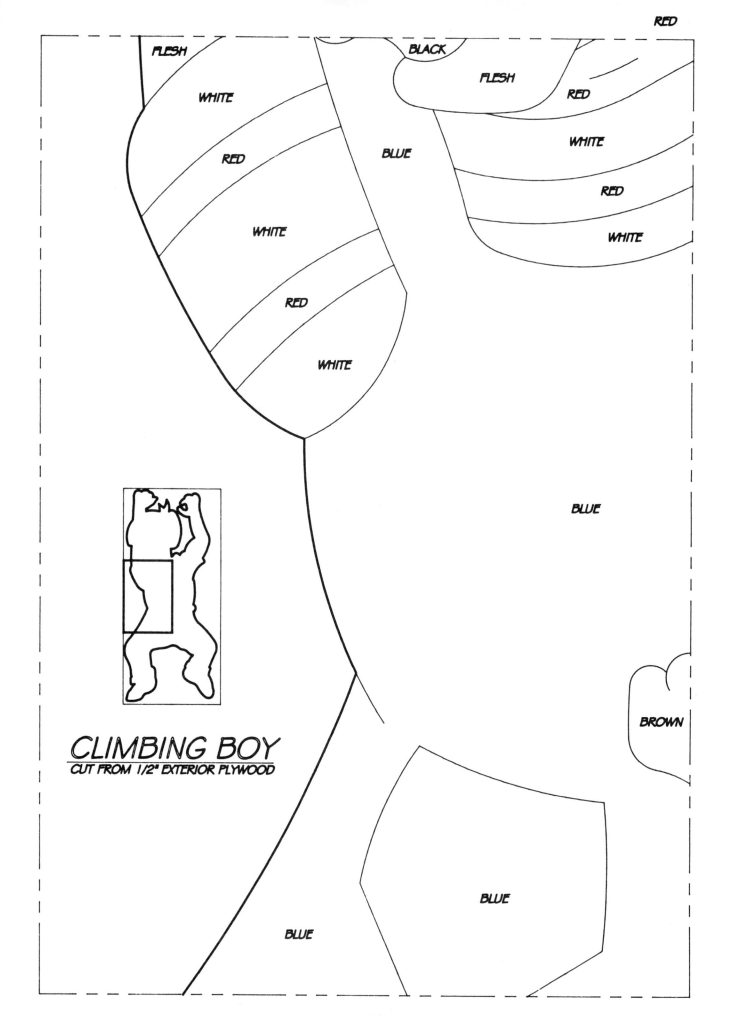

RED

FLESH

BLACK

FLESH

WHITE

RED

RED

WHITE

BLUE

RED

WHITE

WHITE

RED

WHITE

RED

WHITE

BLUE

BLUE

BROWN

CLIMBING BOY
CUT FROM 1/2" EXTERIOR PLYWOOD

BLUE

BLUE

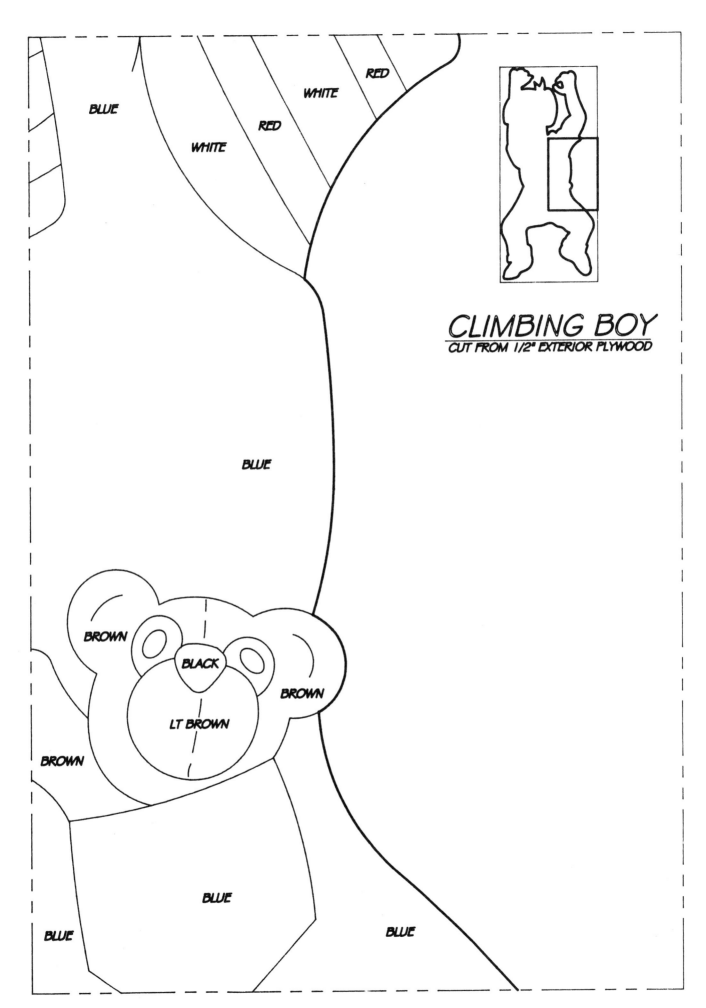

CLIMBING BOY

CUT FROM 1/2" EXTERIOR PLYWOOD

75

FEEDING SQUIRREL
CUT FROM 1/2" EXTERIOR PLYWOOD

CALICO HEN AND CHICK
CUT FROM 1/2" EXTERIOR PLYWOOD

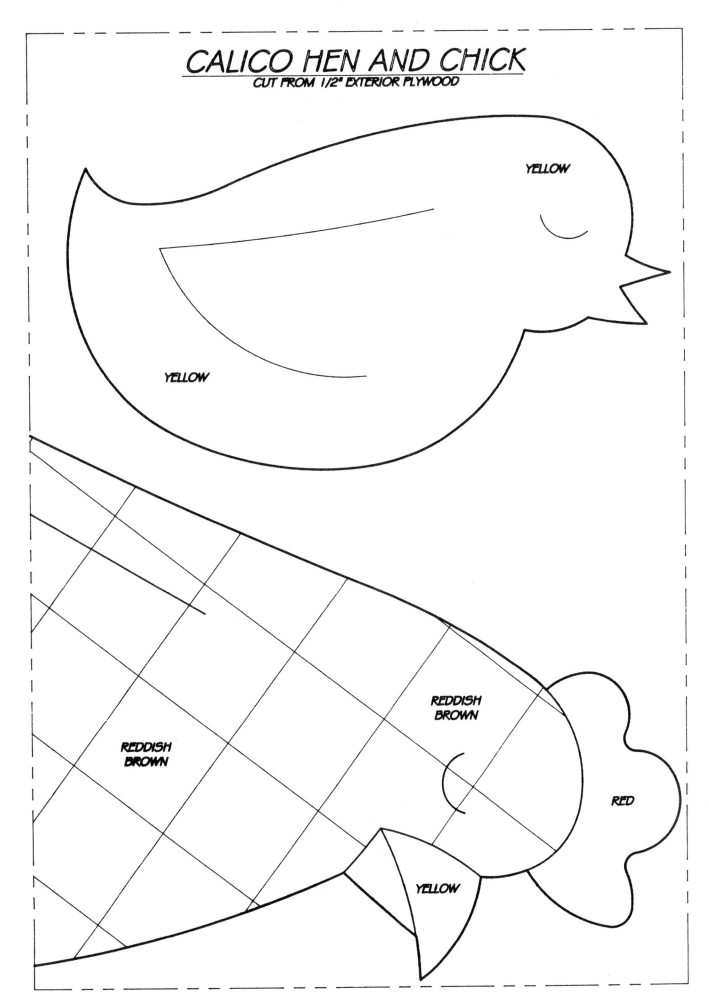

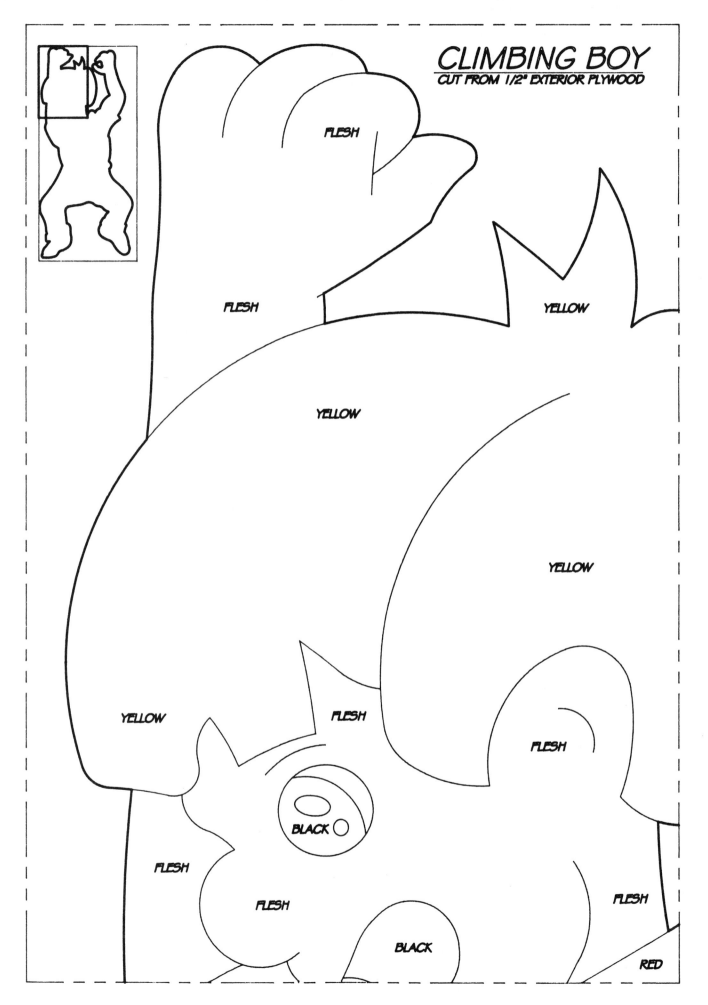

CLIMBING BOY
CUT FROM 1/2" EXTERIOR PLYWOOD

FLESH

FLESH

YELLOW

YELLOW

YELLOW

YELLOW

FLESH

FLESH

BLACK

FLESH

FLESH

FLESH

BLACK

RED

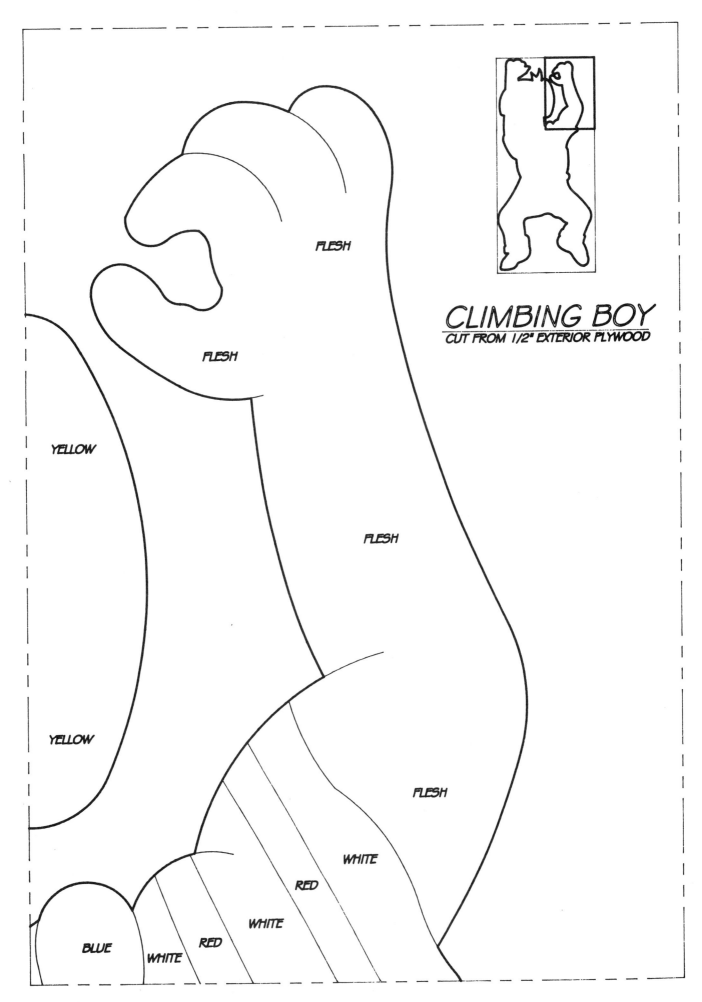

CLIMBING BOY
CUT FROM 1/2" EXTERIOR PLYWOOD

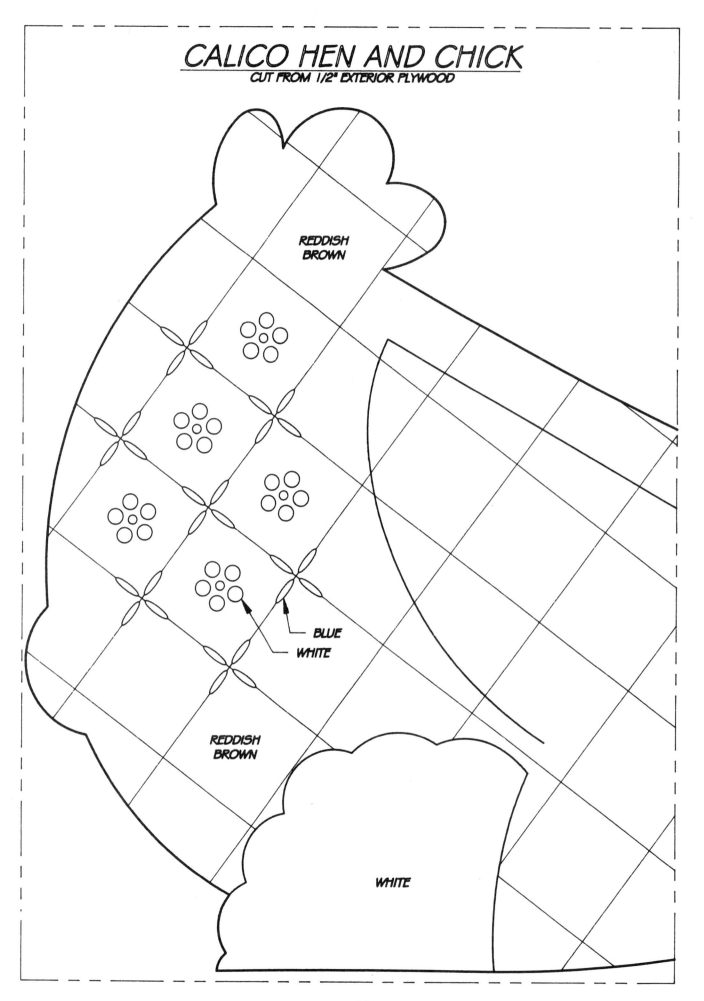

CALICO HEN AND CHICK
CUT FROM 1/2" EXTERIOR PLYWOOD

REDDISH BROWN

BLUE

WHITE

REDDISH BROWN

WHITE

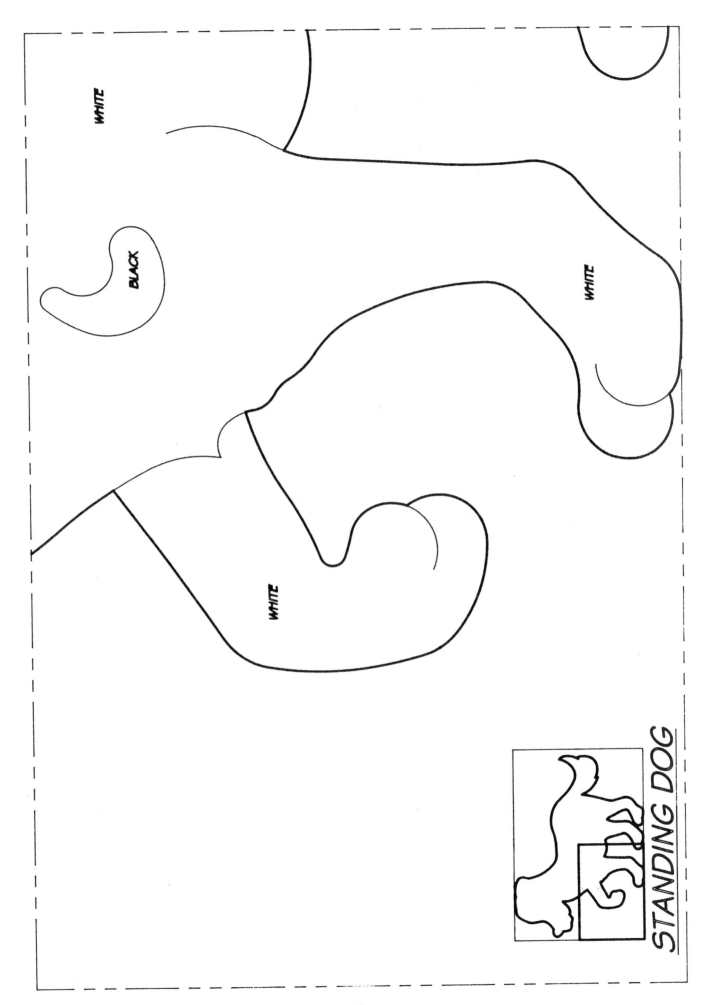

WHITE

BLACK

WHITE

WHITE

STANDING DOG

PAINT PUPIL BLUE OR BLACK.
ALTERNATE SPOTS LIGHT
BROWN AND BLACK.

RUNNING DOG

LT BROWN

WHITE

LT BROWN

LT BROWN

WHITE

WHITE

BLACK

BLACK

BLACK

RED

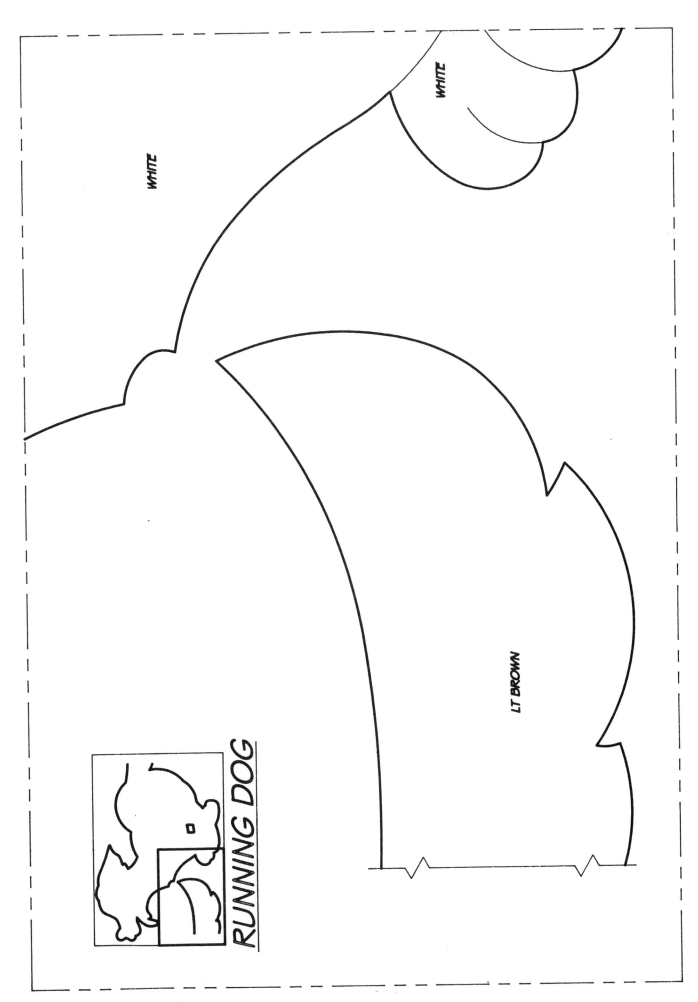

WHITE

WHITE

LT BROWN

RUNNING DOG

STANDING DOG

BLACK

WHITE

LT BROWN

LT BROWN

WHITE

LT BROWN

BLACK

PAINT PUPIL BLUE OR BLACK.
ALTERNATE SPOTS LIGHT
BROWN AND BLACK.

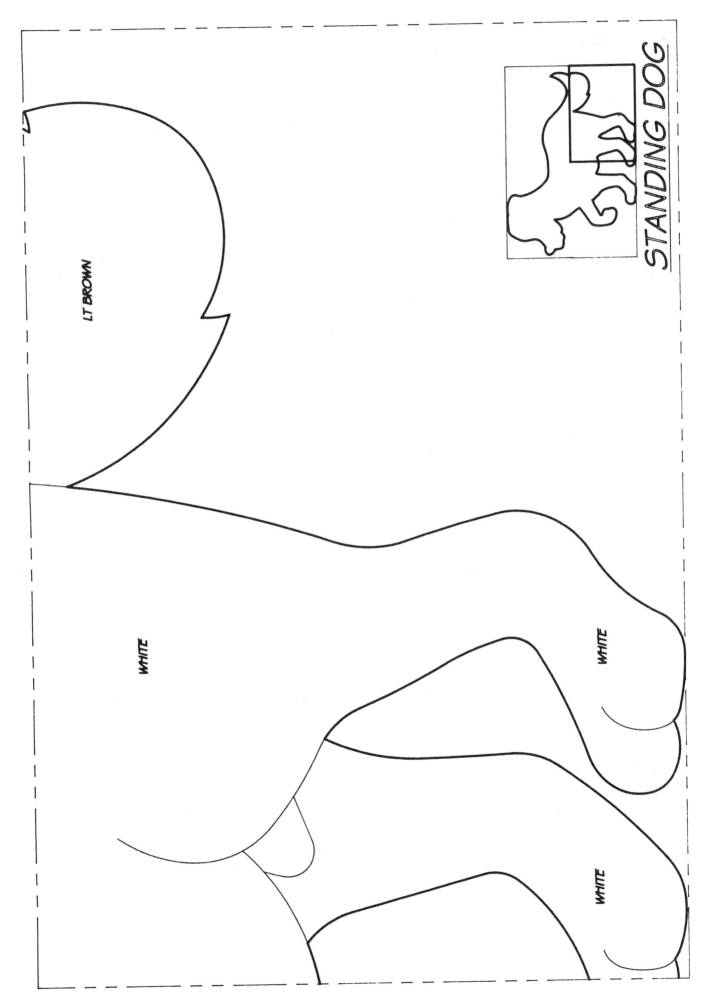

LT BROWN

WHITE

WHITE

WHITE

STANDING DOG

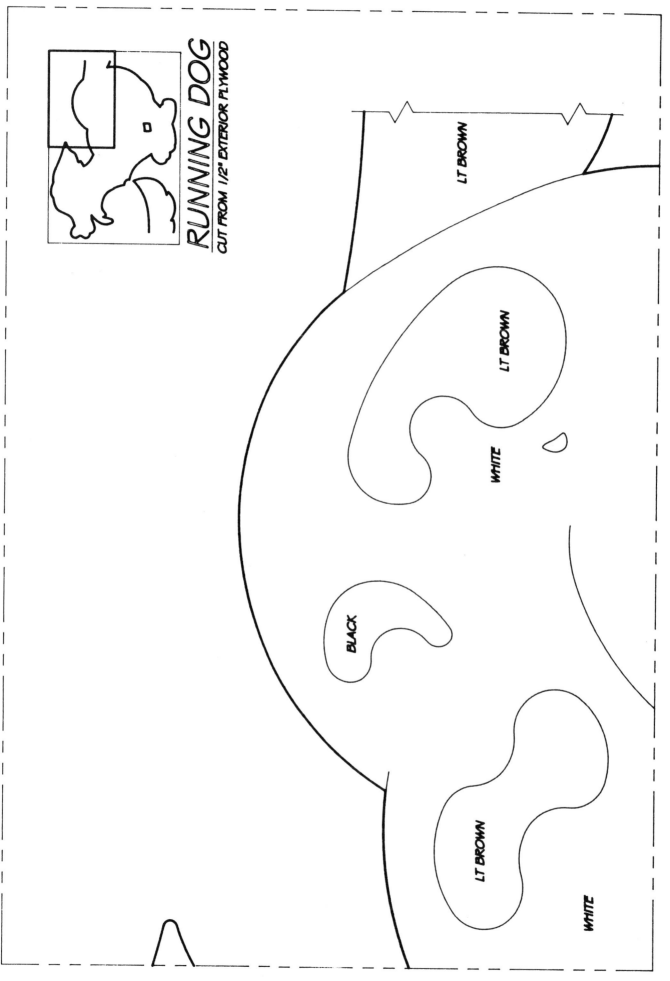

RUNNING DOG
CUT FROM 1/2" EXTERIOR PLYWOOD

LT BROWN

LT BROWN

WHITE

BLACK

LT BROWN

WHITE

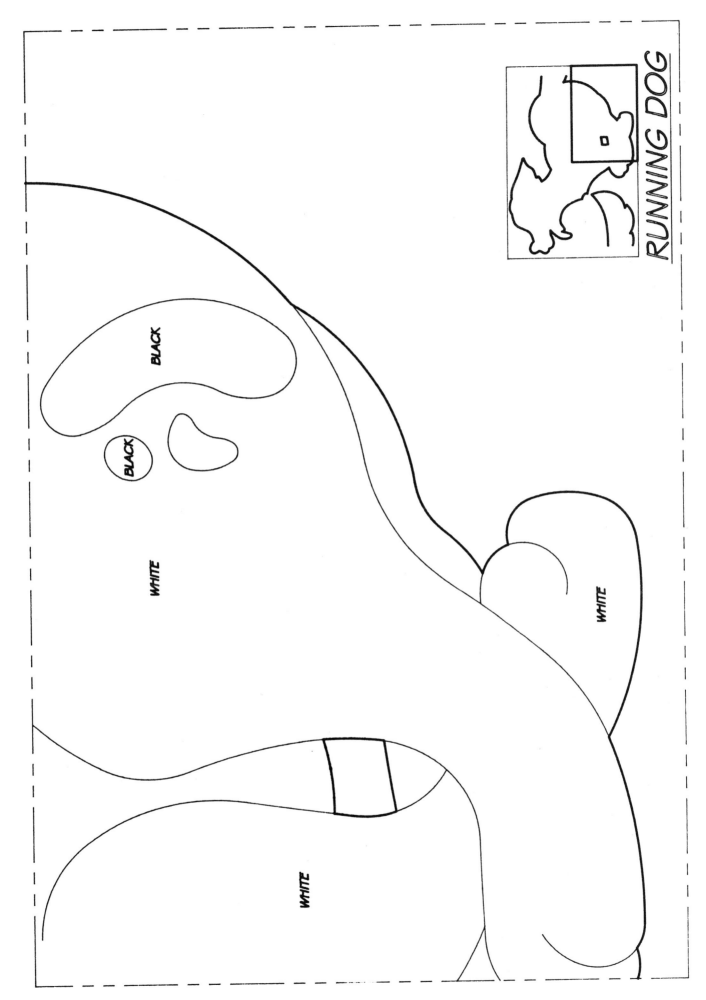

RUNNING DOG

BLACK

BLACK

WHITE

WHITE

WHITE

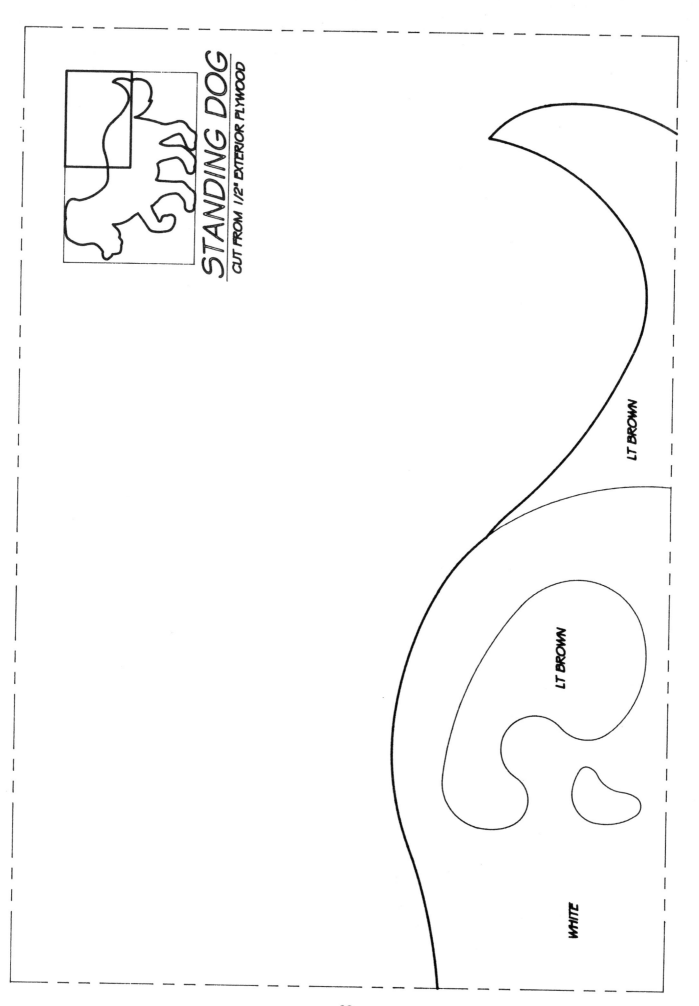

STANDING DOG
CUT FROM 1/2" EXTERIOR PLYWOOD

LT BROWN

LT BROWN

WHITE

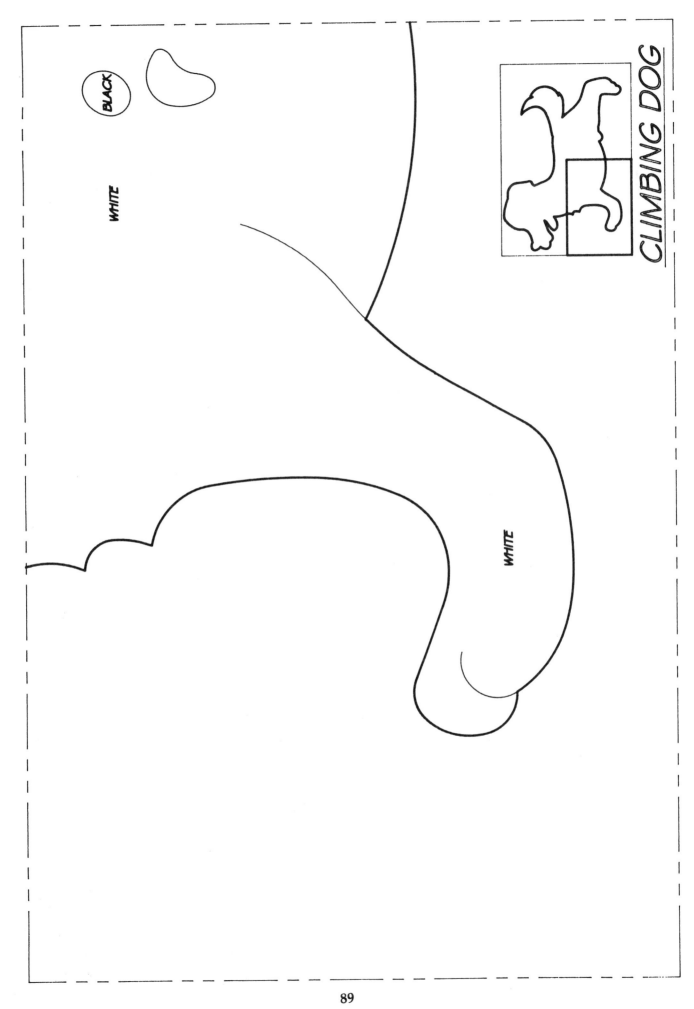

BLACK

WHITE

WHITE

CLIMBING DOG

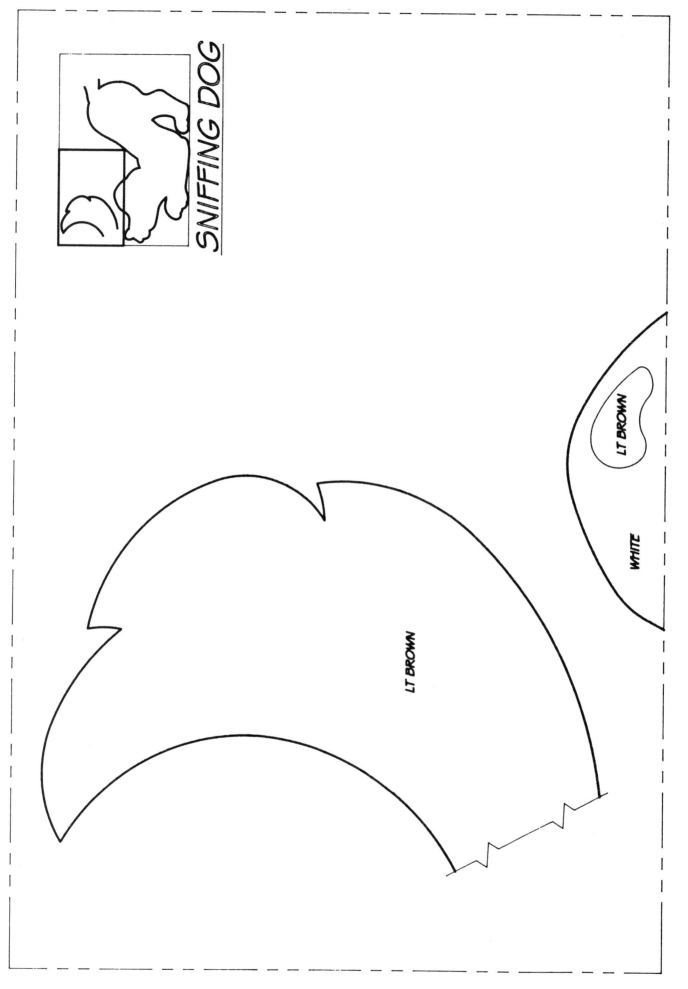

SNIFFING DOG

LT BROWN

WHITE

LT BROWN

90

WHITE

LT BROWN

LT BROWN

LT BROWN

WHITE

WHITE

BLACK

BLACK

LT BROWN

PAINT PUPIL BLUE OR BLACK.
ALTERNATE SPOTS LIGHT
BROWN AND BLACK.

SNIFFING DOG

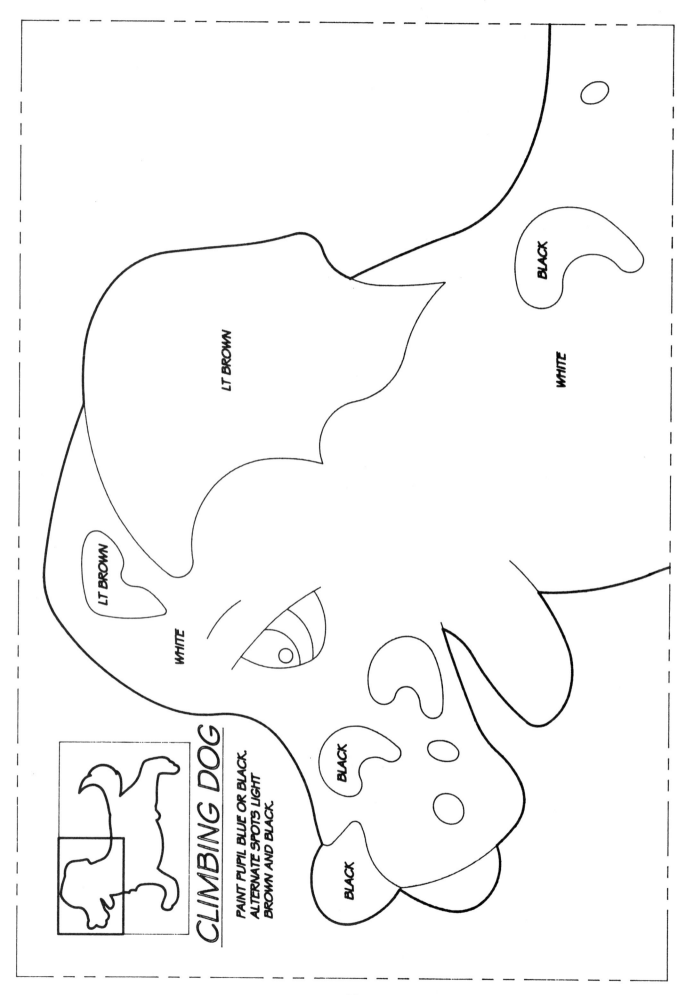

CLIMBING DOG

PAINT PUPIL BLUE OR BLACK.
ALTERNATE SPOTS LIGHT
BROWN AND BLACK.

LT BROWN

BLACK

WHITE

LT BROWN

WHITE

BLACK

BLACK

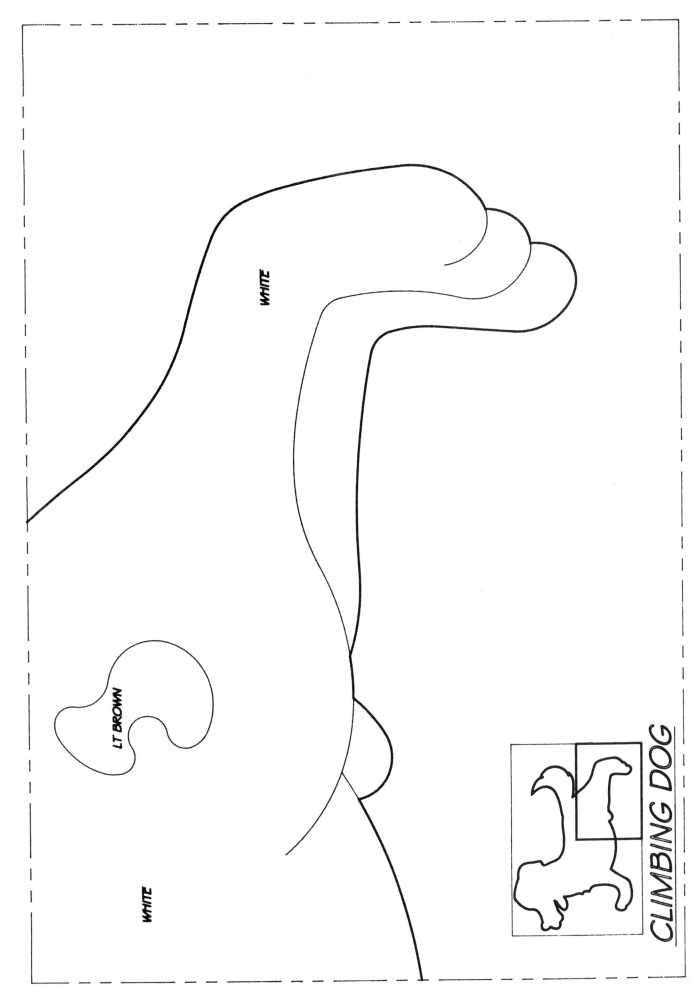

WHITE

LT BROWN

WHITE

CLIMBING DOG

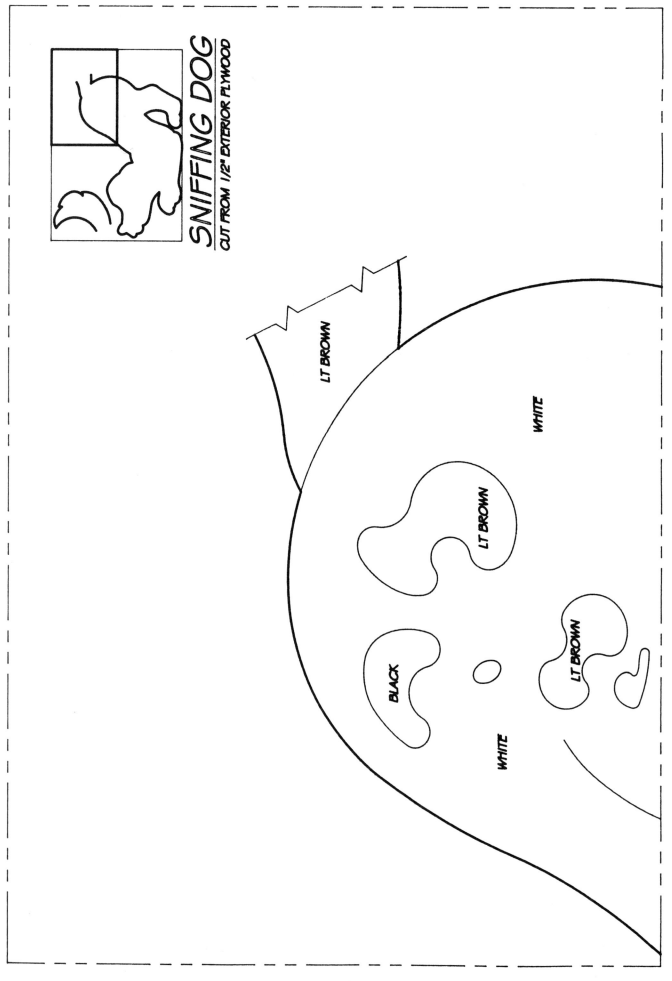

SNIFFING DOG
CUT FROM 1/2" EXTERIOR PLYWOOD

LT BROWN

WHITE

LT BROWN

BLACK

LT BROWN

WHITE

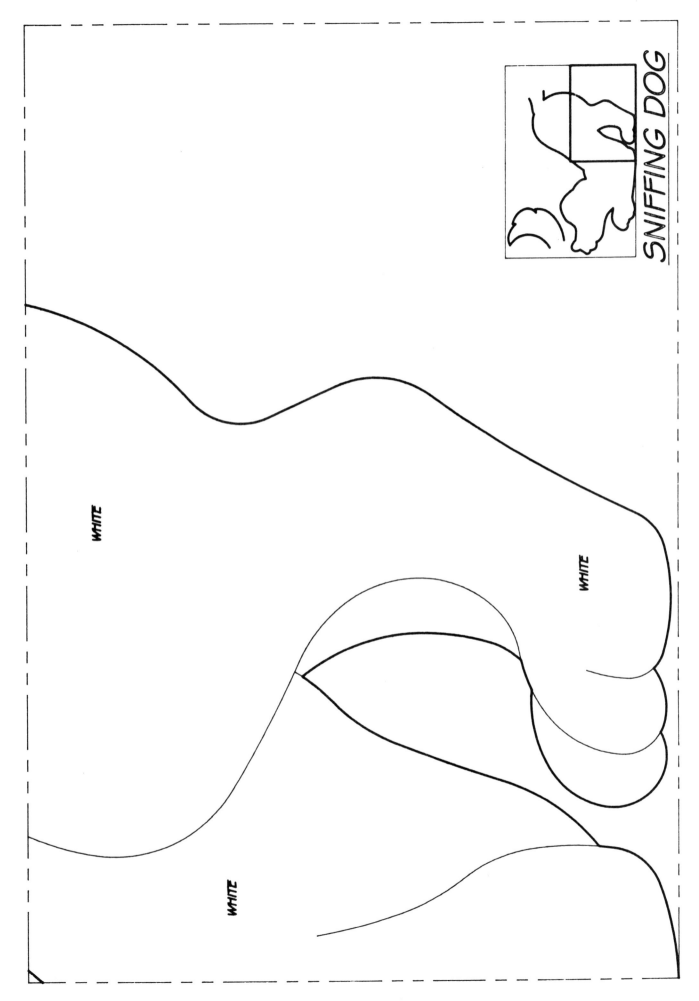

SNIFFING DOG

WHITE

WHITE

WHITE

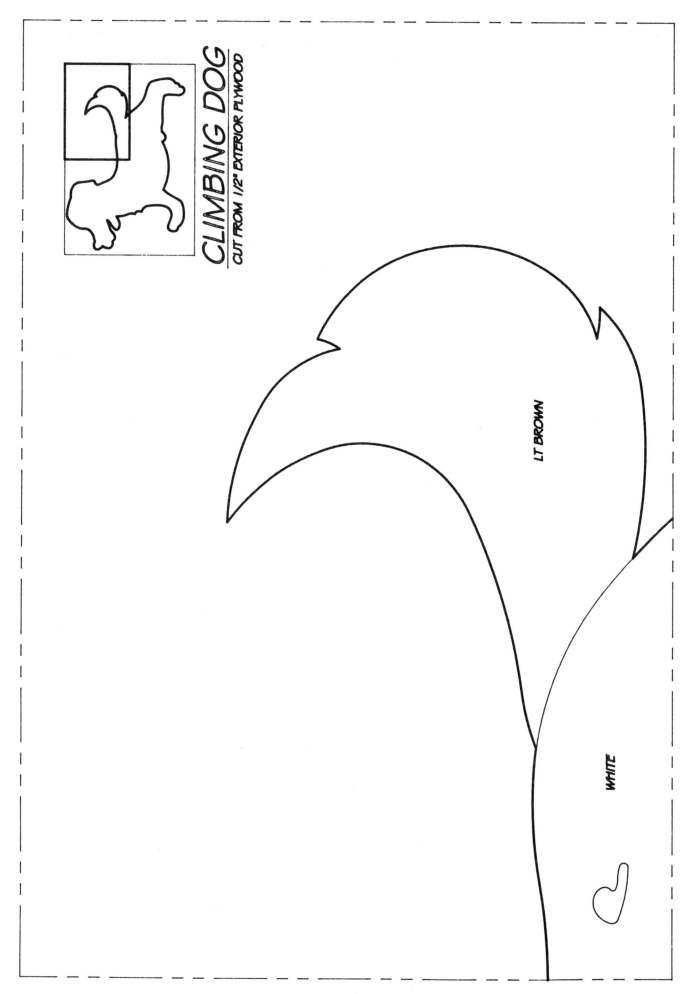

CLIMBING DOG
CUT FROM 1/2" EXTERIOR PLYWOOD

LT BROWN

WHITE

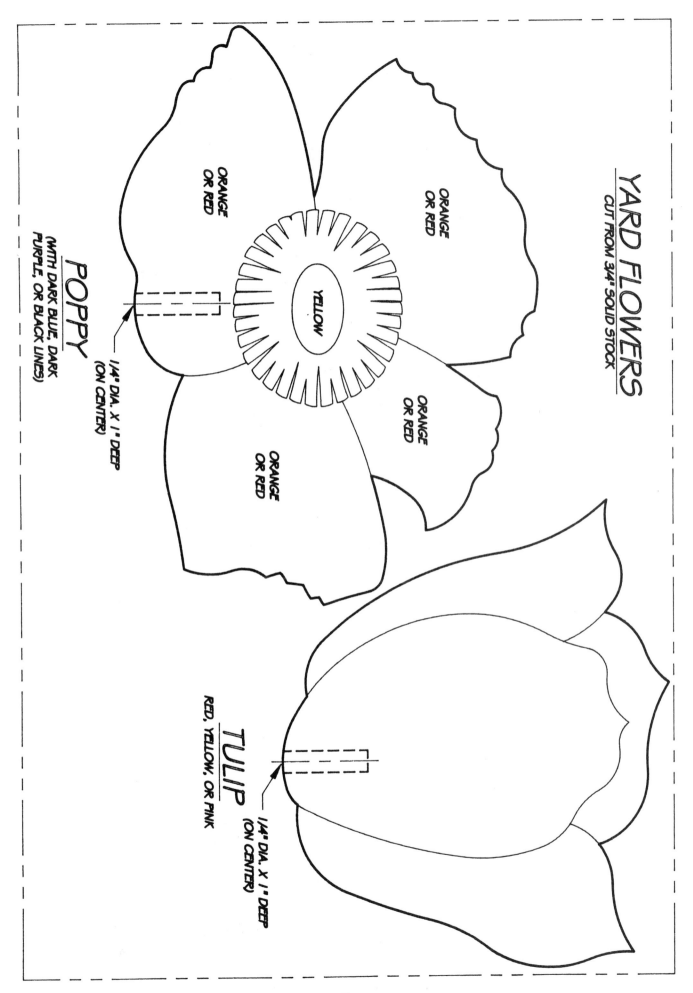

YARD FLOWERS
CUT FROM 3/4" SOLID STOCK

ORANGE OR RED

ORANGE OR RED

YELLOW

ORANGE OR RED

ORANGE OR RED

POPPY
(WITH DARK BLUE, DARK PURPLE, OR BLACK LINES)

1/4" DIA. X 1" DEEP (ON CENTER)

TULIP
RED, YELLOW, OR PINK

1/4" DIA. X 1" DEEP (ON CENTER)

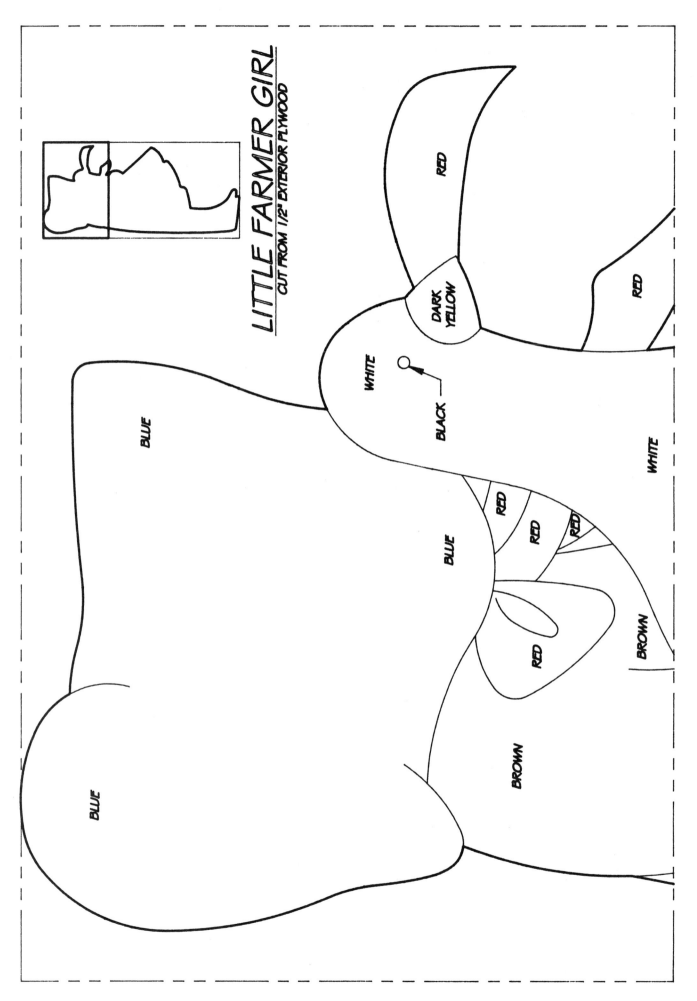

LITTLE FARMER GIRL
CUT FROM 1/2" EXTERIOR PLYWOOD

RED

RED

DARK YELLOW

WHITE

BLACK

BLUE

WHITE

BLUE

BLUE

RED

RED

RED

RED

BROWN

BROWN

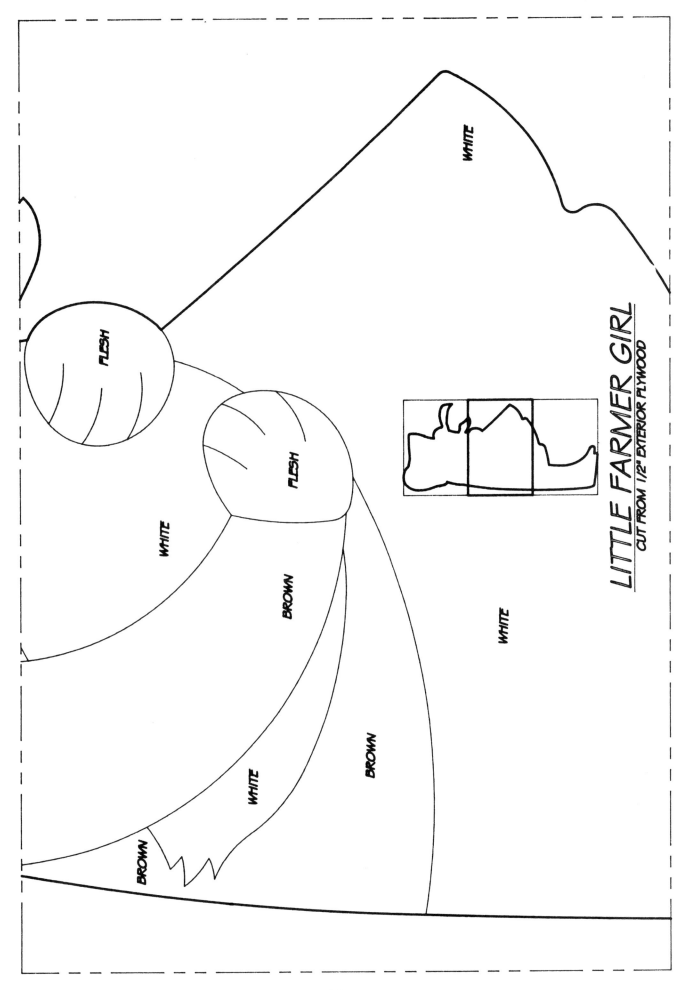

LITTLE FARMER GIRL
CUT FROM 1/2" EXTERIOR PLYWOOD

WHITE

FLESH

FLESH

WHITE

BROWN

BROWN

WHITE

WHITE

BROWN

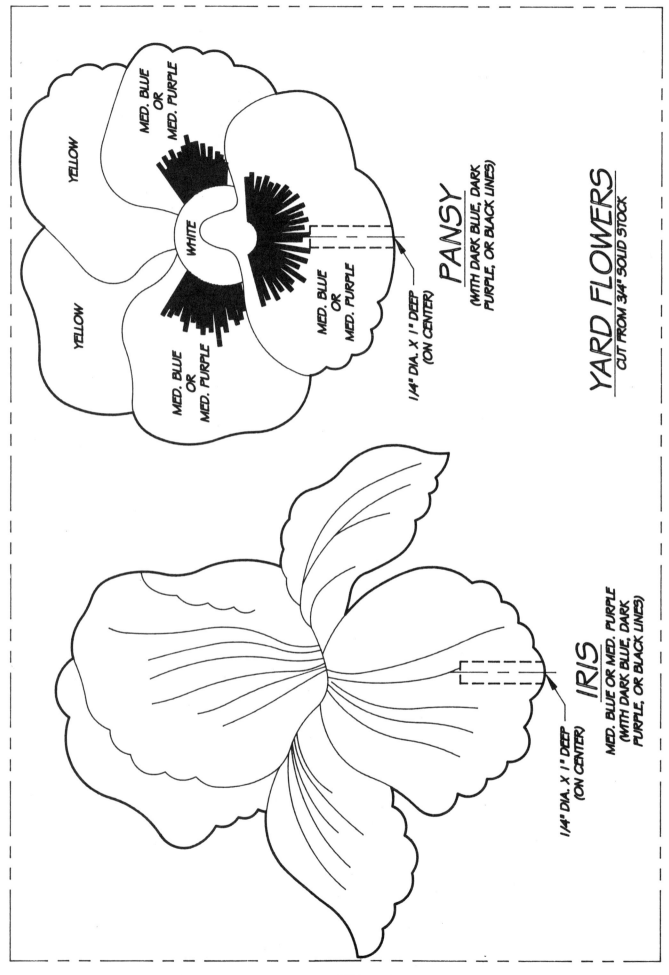

PANSY
(WITH DARK BLUE, DARK
PURPLE, OR BLACK LINES)

YELLOW

YELLOW

MED. BLUE
OR
MED. PURPLE

WHITE

MED. BLUE
OR
MED. PURPLE

MED. BLUE
OR
MED. PURPLE

1/4" DIA. X 1" DEEP
(ON CENTER)

YARD FLOWERS
CUT FROM 3/4" SOLID STOCK

IRIS
MED. BLUE OR MED. PURPLE
(WITH DARK BLUE, DARK
PURPLE, OR BLACK LINES)

1/4" DIA. X 1" DEEP
(ON CENTER)

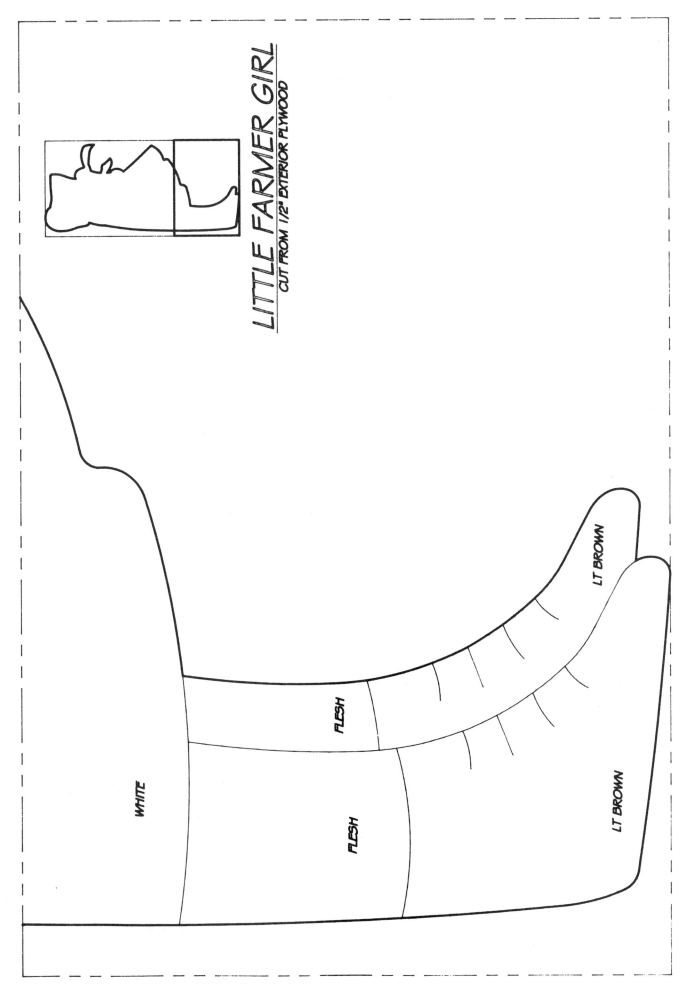

LITTLE FARMER GIRL
CUT FROM 1/2" EXTERIOR PLYWOOD

WHITE

FLESH

FLESH

LT BROWN

LT BROWN

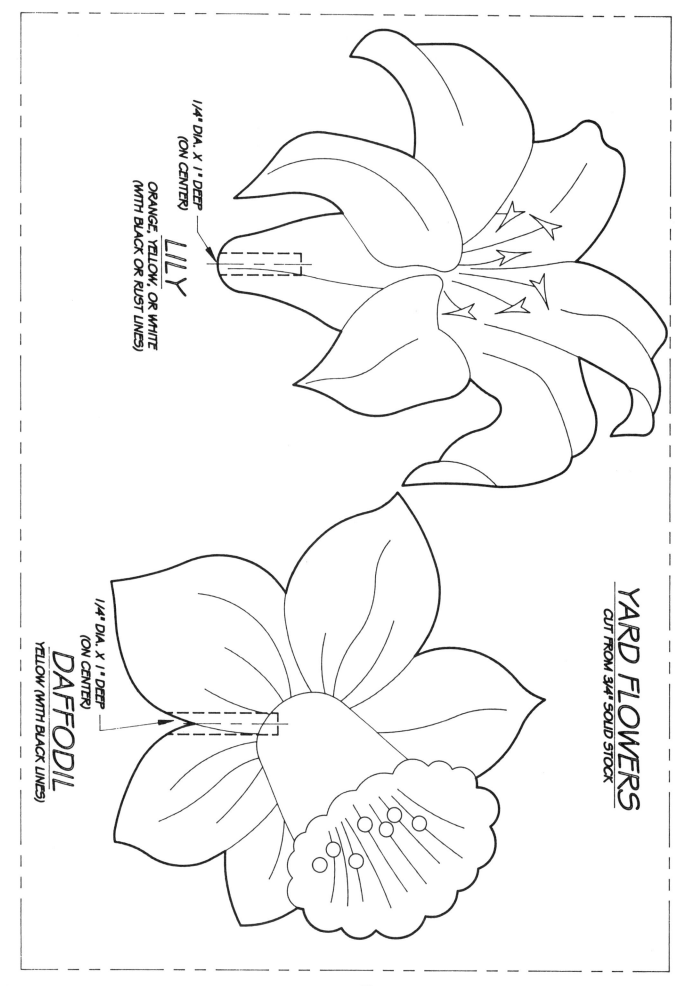

YARD FLOWERS
CUT FROM 3/4" SOLID STOCK

1/4" DIA. X 1" DEEP
(ON CENTER)
LILY
ORANGE, YELLOW, OR WHITE
(WITH BLACK OR RUST LINES)

1/4" DIA. X 1" DEEP
(ON CENTER)
DAFFODIL
YELLOW (WITH BLACK LINES)

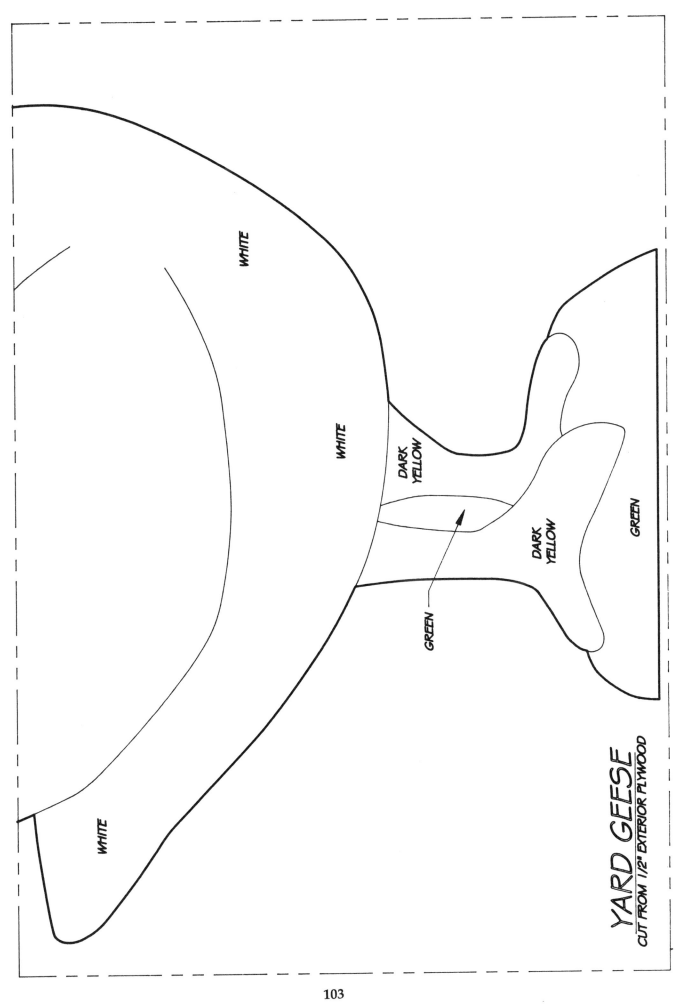

WHITE

WHITE

WHITE

DARK YELLOW

DARK YELLOW

GREEN

GREEN

YARD GEESE
CUT FROM 1/2" EXTERIOR PLYWOOD

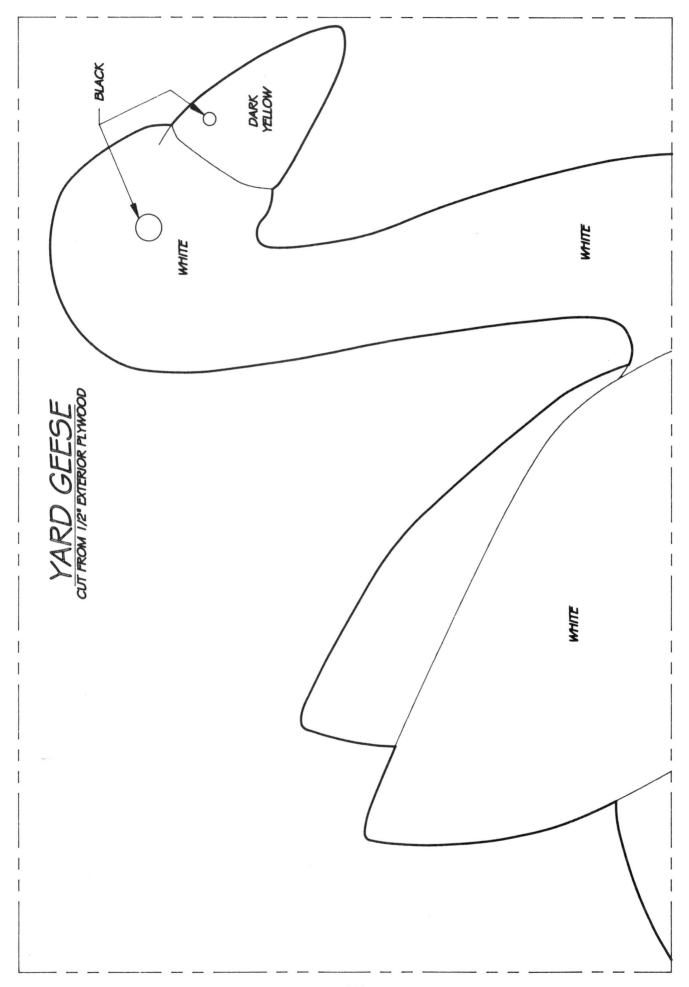

YARD GEESE
CUT FROM 1/2" EXTERIOR PLYWOOD

BLACK

DARK
YELLOW

WHITE

WHITE

WHITE

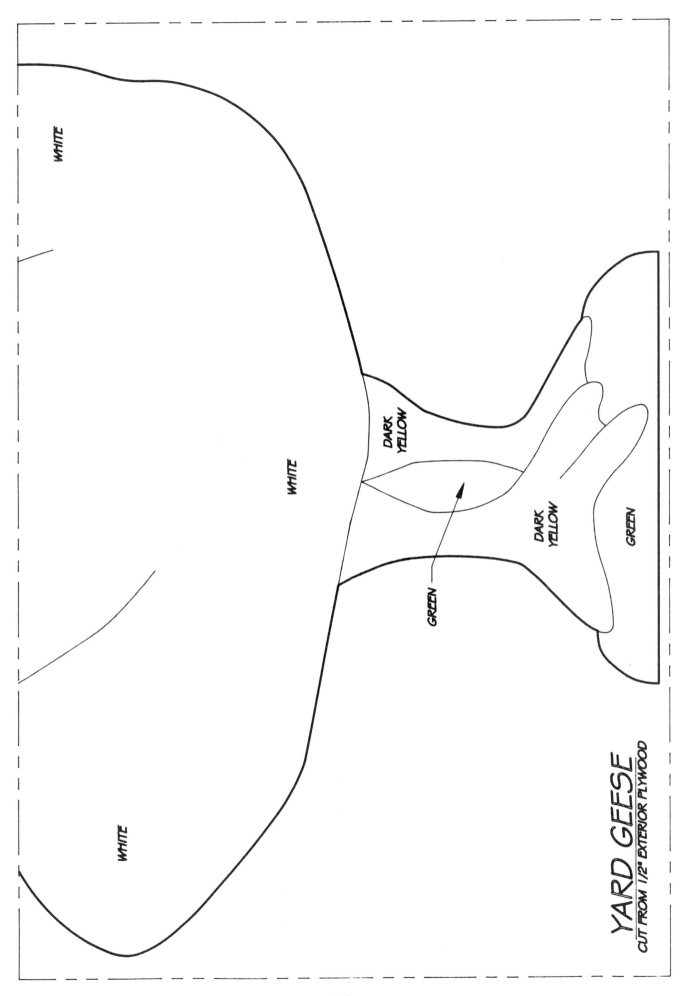

WHITE

WHITE

WHITE

WHITE

DARK YELLOW

DARK YELLOW

GREEN

GREEN

YARD GEESE
CUT FROM 1/2" EXTERIOR PLYWOOD

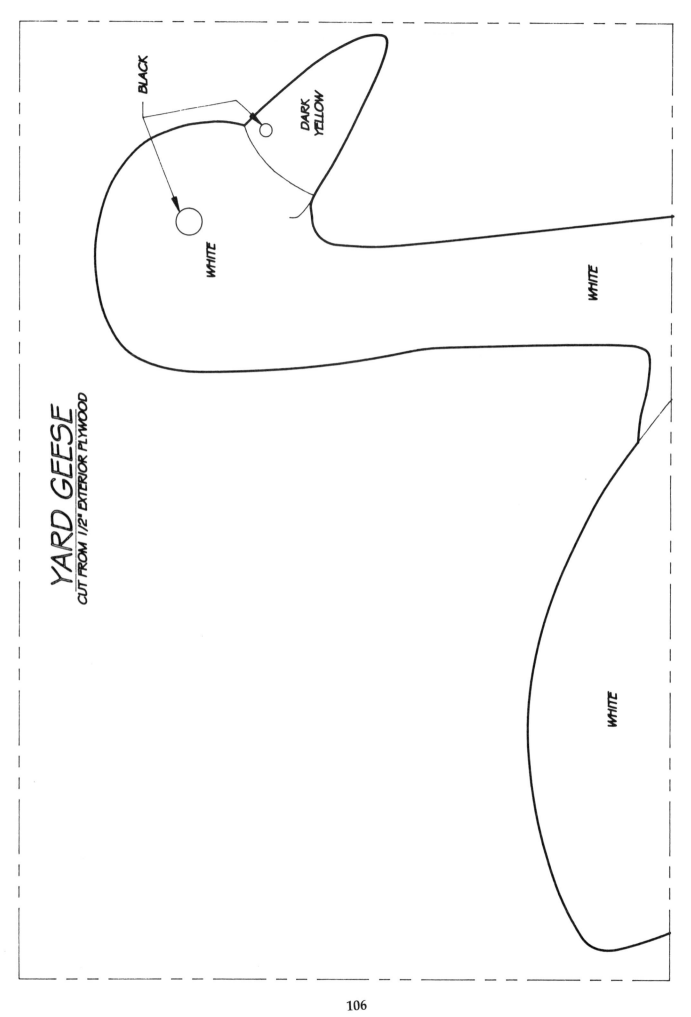

YARD GEESE
CUT FROM 1/2" EXTERIOR PLYWOOD

BLACK

DARK YELLOW

WHITE

WHITE

WHITE

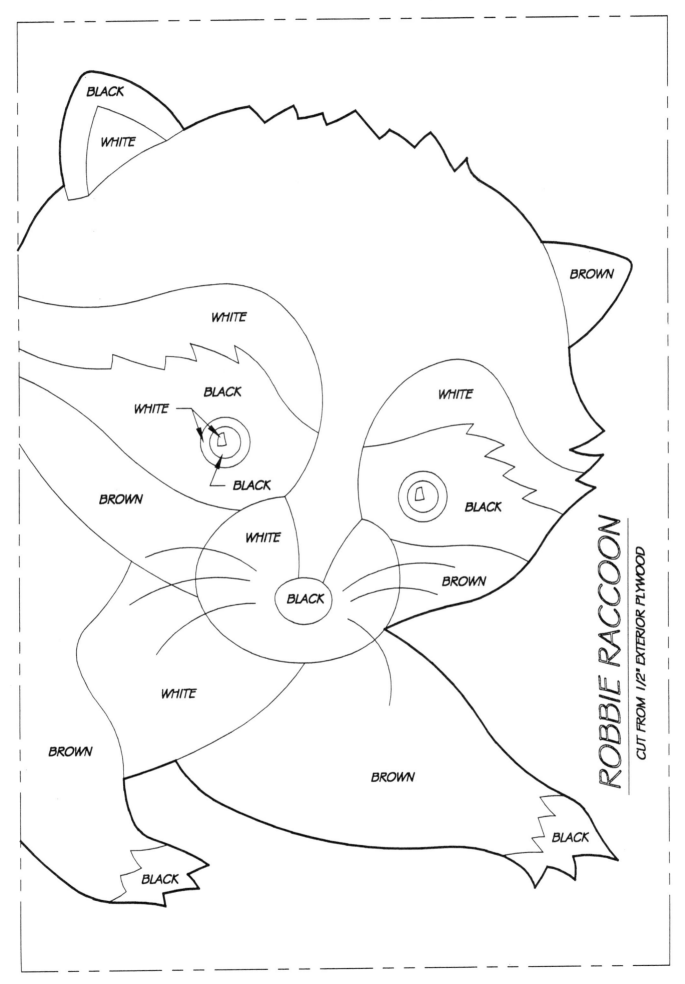

RUNNING CAT
CUT FROM 1/2" EXTERIOR PLYWOOD

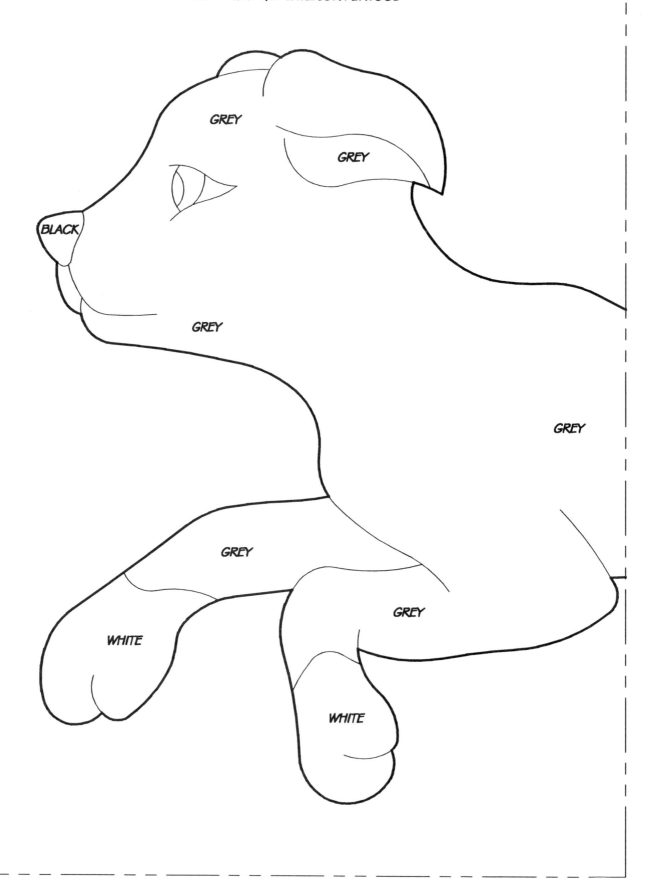

GREY

GREY

BLACK

GREY

GREY

GREY

WHITE

GREY

WHITE

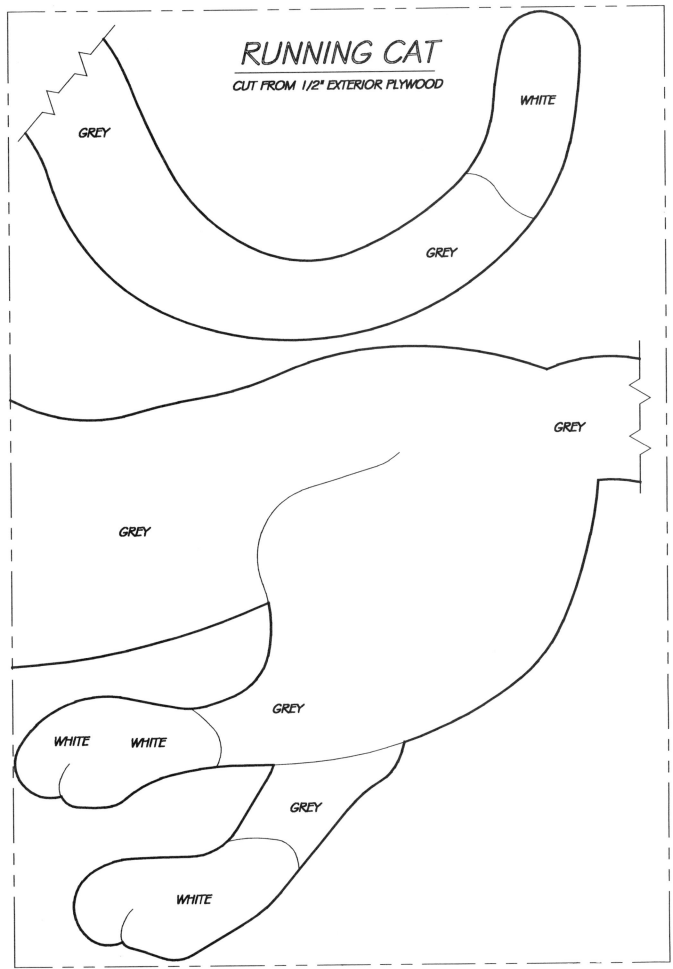

RUNNING CAT

CUT FROM 1/2" EXTERIOR PLYWOOD

WHITE

GREY

GREY

GREY

GREY

GREY

GREY

GREY

WHITE   WHITE

WHITE

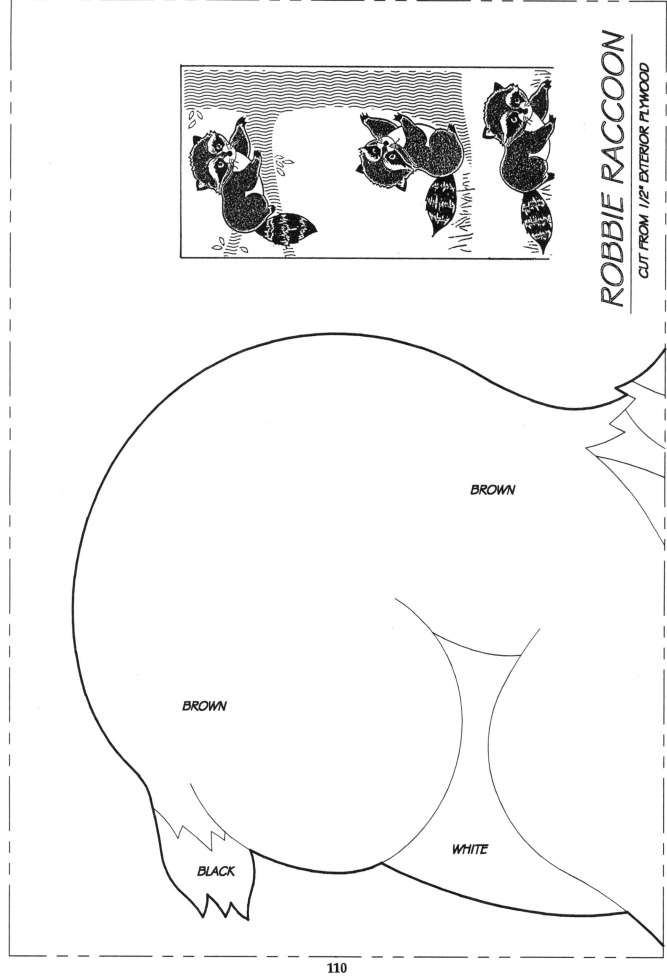

ROBBIE RACCOON

CUT FROM 1/2" EXTERIOR PLYWOOD

BROWN

BROWN

WHITE

BLACK

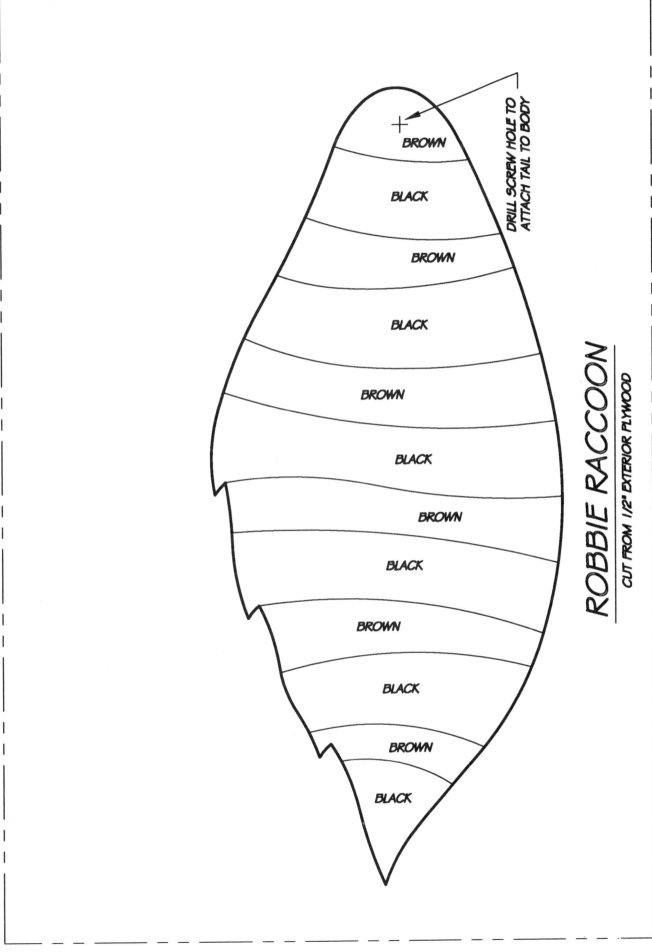

BROWN

BLACK

BROWN

BLACK

BROWN

BLACK

BROWN

BLACK

BROWN

BLACK

BROWN

BLACK

DRILL SCREW HOLE TO
ATTACH TAIL TO BODY

ROBBIE RACCOON
CUT FROM 1/2" EXTERIOR PLYWOOD

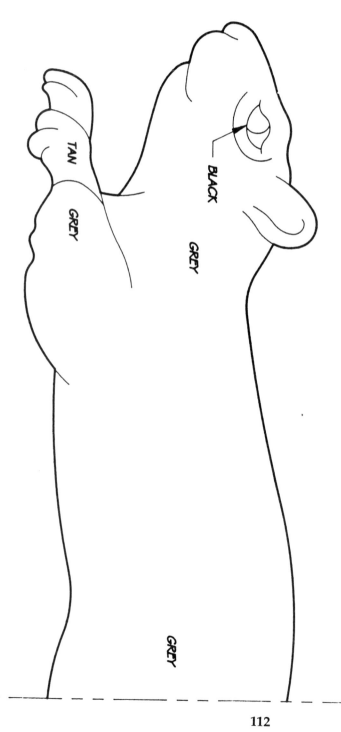

RUNNING SQUIRREL
CUT FROM 1/2" EXTERIOR PLYWOOD

BLACK

TAN

GREY

GREY

GREY

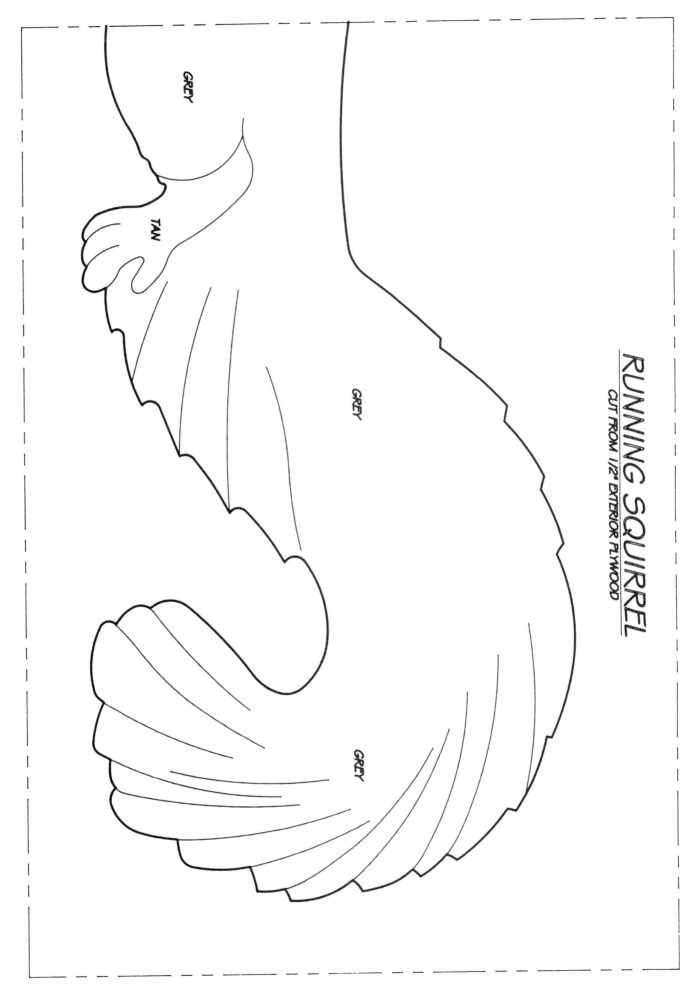

GREY

TAN

GREY

GREY

RUNNING SQUIRREL
CUT FROM 1/2" EXTERIOR PLYWOOD

YARD BIRDS

CUT FROM 3/4" SOLID STOCK

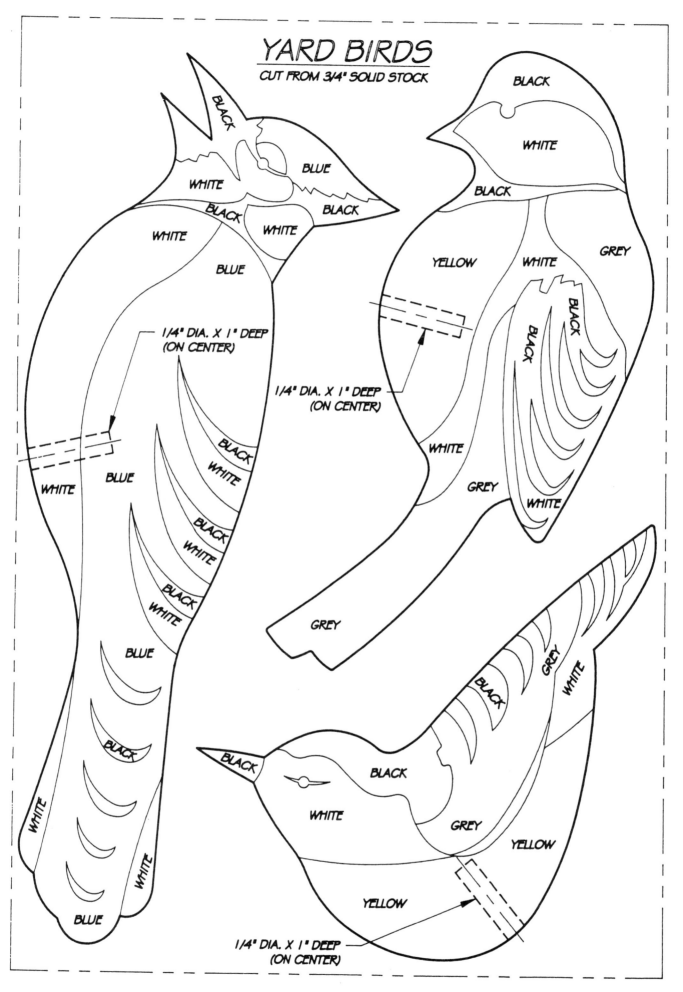

BLACK

BLUE

WHITE

BLACK

BLACK

WHITE

BLUE

1/4" DIA. X 1" DEEP
(ON CENTER)

1/4" DIA. X 1" DEEP
(ON CENTER)

BLACK
WHITE

BLUE

WHITE

BLACK
WHITE

BLACK
WHITE

BLUE

BLACK

WHITE

WHITE

BLUE

BLACK

WHITE

BLACK

WHITE

YELLOW

WHITE

GREY

BLACK

BLACK

WHITE

GREY

WHITE

GREY

BLACK

GREY

WHITE

BLACK

BLACK

WHITE

GREY

YELLOW

YELLOW

1/4" DIA. X 1" DEEP
(ON CENTER)

114

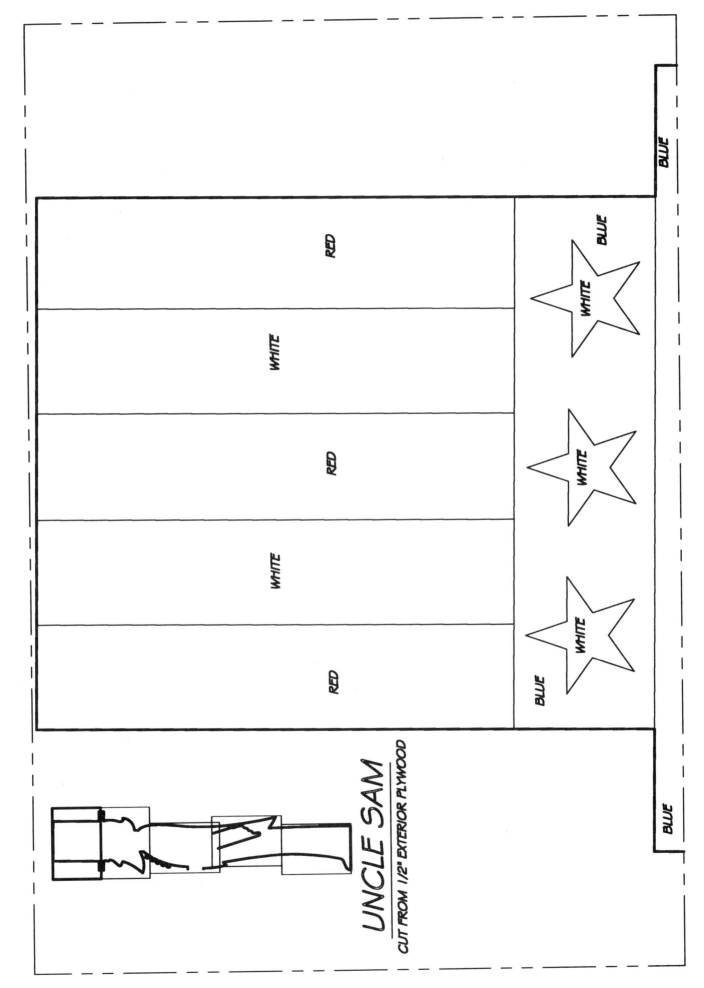

UNCLE SAM

CUT FROM 1/2" EXTERIOR PLYWOOD

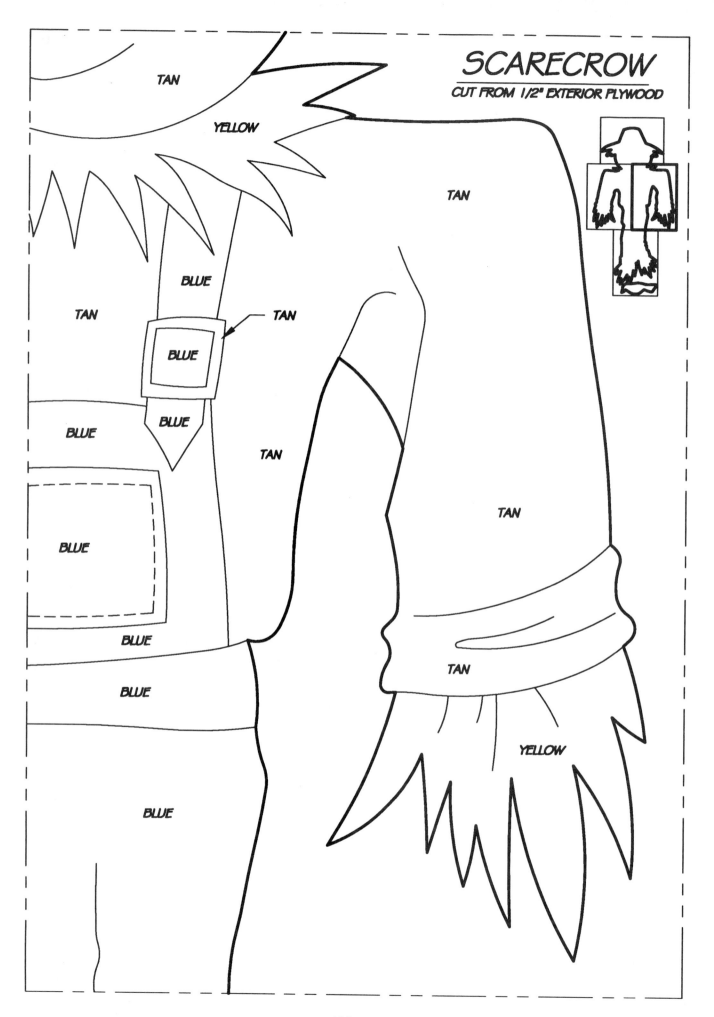

SCARECROW
CUT FROM 1/2" EXTERIOR PLYWOOD

TAN

YELLOW

TAN

BLUE

TAN

TAN

BLUE

BLUE

BLUE

BLUE

BLUE

TAN

TAN

TAN

TAN

YELLOW

BLUE

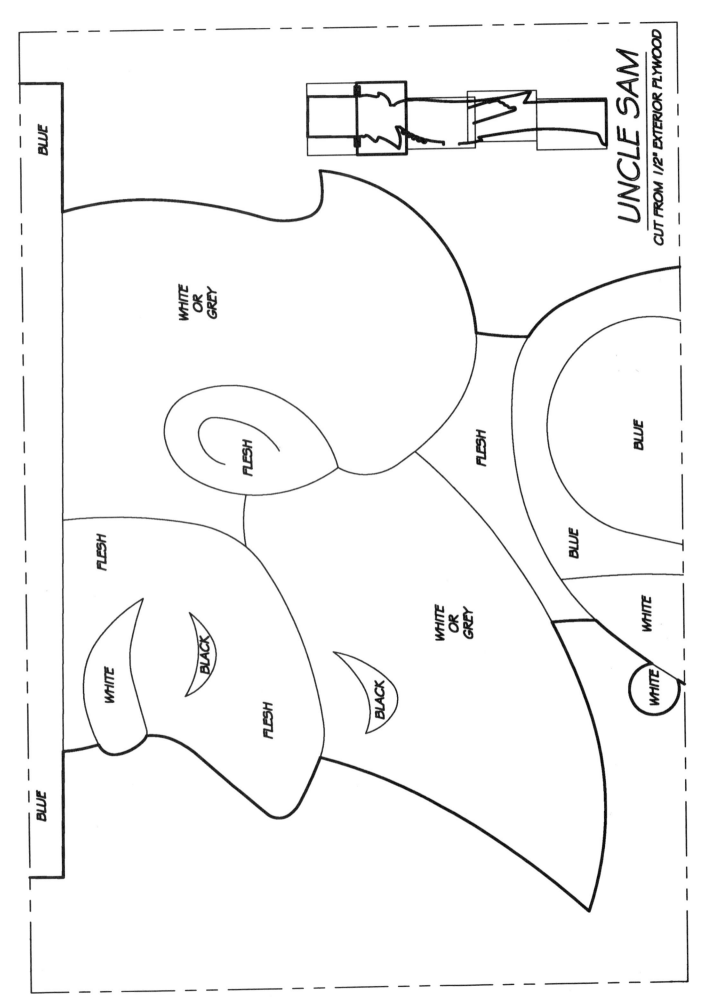

UNCLE SAM

CUT FROM 1/2" EXTERIOR PLYWOOD

BLUE

BLUE

WHITE OR GREY

FLESH

FLESH

BLUE

BLUE

WHITE

FLESH

WHITE

BLACK

FLESH

BLACK

WHITE OR GREY

WHITE

WHITE

SCARECROW
CUT FROM 1/2" EXTERIOR PLYWOOD

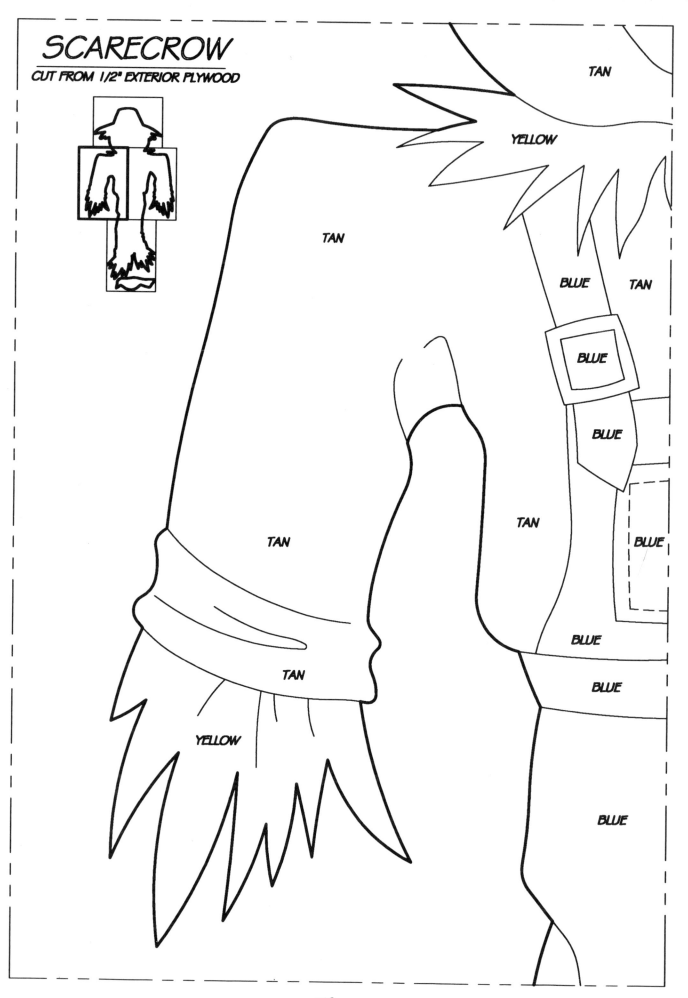

TAN

YELLOW

TAN

BLUE

TAN

BLUE

BLUE

TAN

BLUE

TAN

TAN

BLUE

BLUE

TAN

YELLOW

BLUE

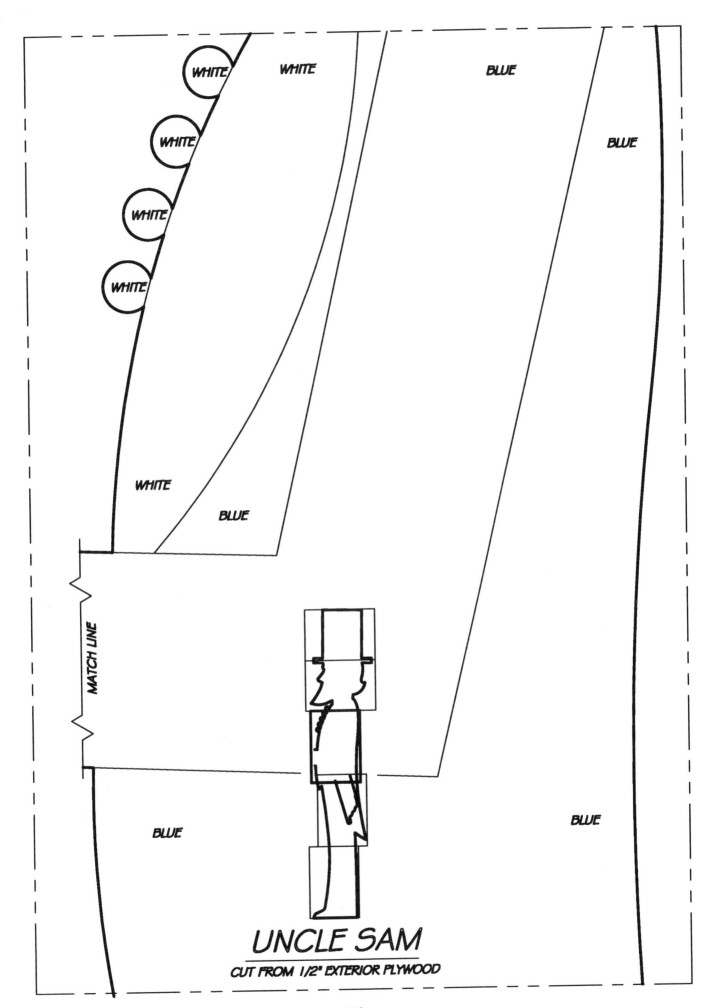

WHITE WHITE WHITE WHITE

WHITE WHITE BLUE BLUE

WHITE BLUE

MATCH LINE

BLUE BLUE

UNCLE SAM
CUT FROM 1/2" EXTERIOR PLYWOOD

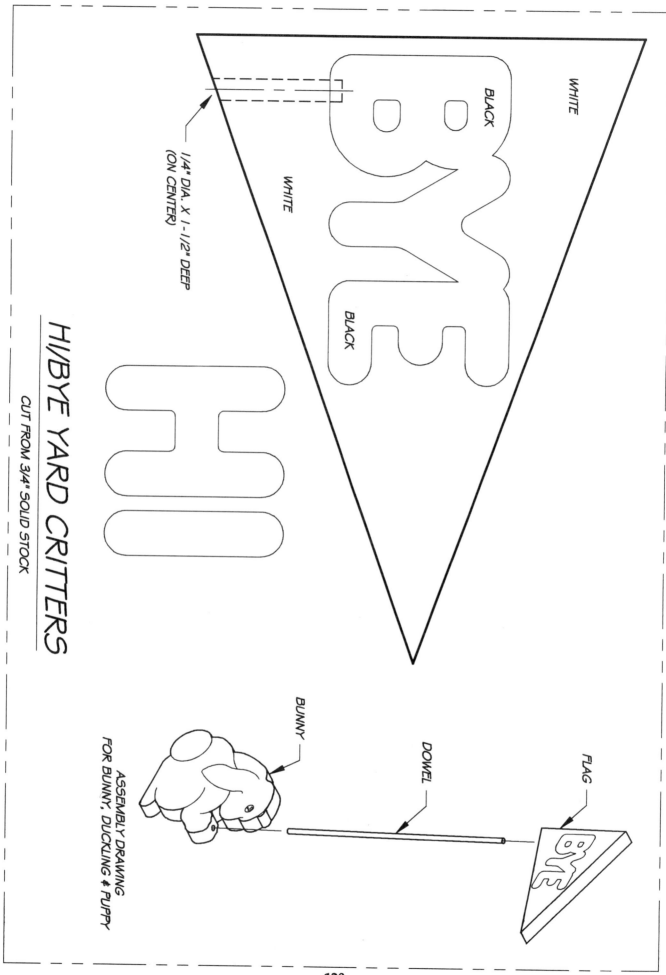

BYE

WHITE

BLACK

WHITE

BLACK

1/4" DIA. X 1-1/2" DEEP
(ON CENTER)

HI

HI/BYE YARD CRITTERS

CUT FROM 3/4" SOLID STOCK

BUNNY

DOWEL

FLAG

ASSEMBLY DRAWING
FOR BUNNY, DUCKLING & PUPPY

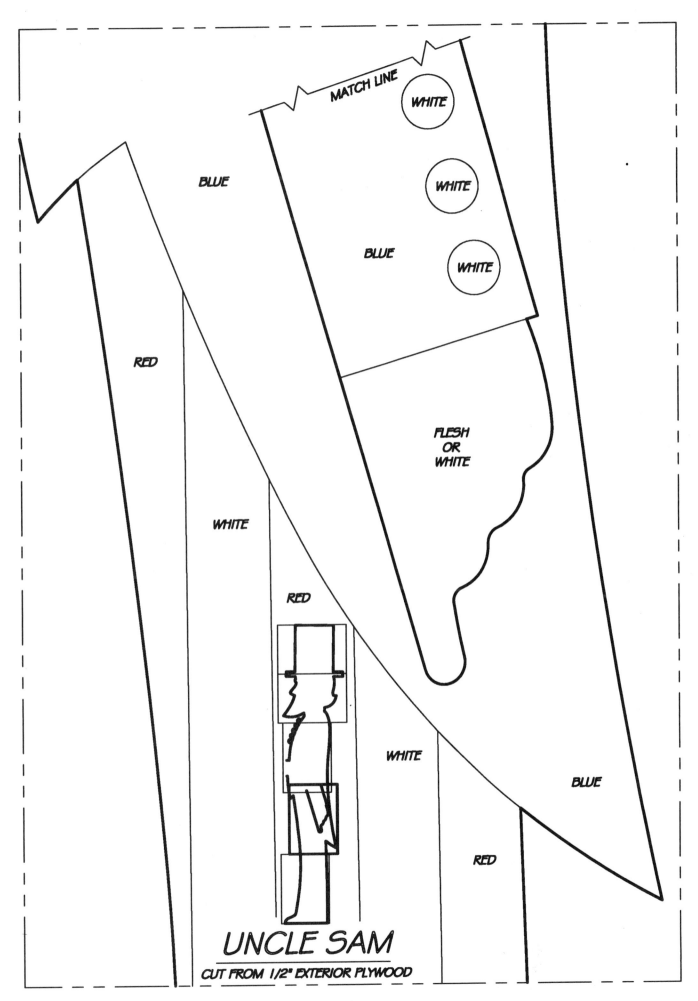

MATCH LINE

WHITE

BLUE

WHITE

BLUE

WHITE

RED

FLESH
OR
WHITE

WHITE

RED

WHITE

BLUE

RED

UNCLE SAM
CUT FROM 1/2" EXTERIOR PLYWOOD

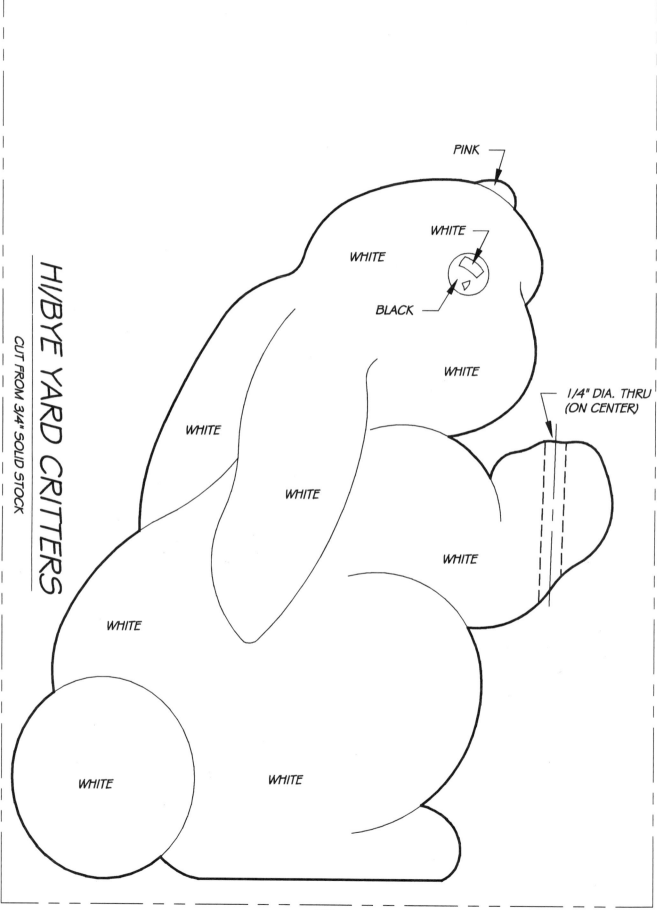

PINK

WHITE

WHITE

WHITE

BLACK

WHITE

1/4" DIA. THRU
(ON CENTER)

WHITE

WHITE

WHITE

WHITE

WHITE

WHITE

WHITE

HI/BYE YARD CRITTERS

CUT FROM 3/4" SOLID STOCK

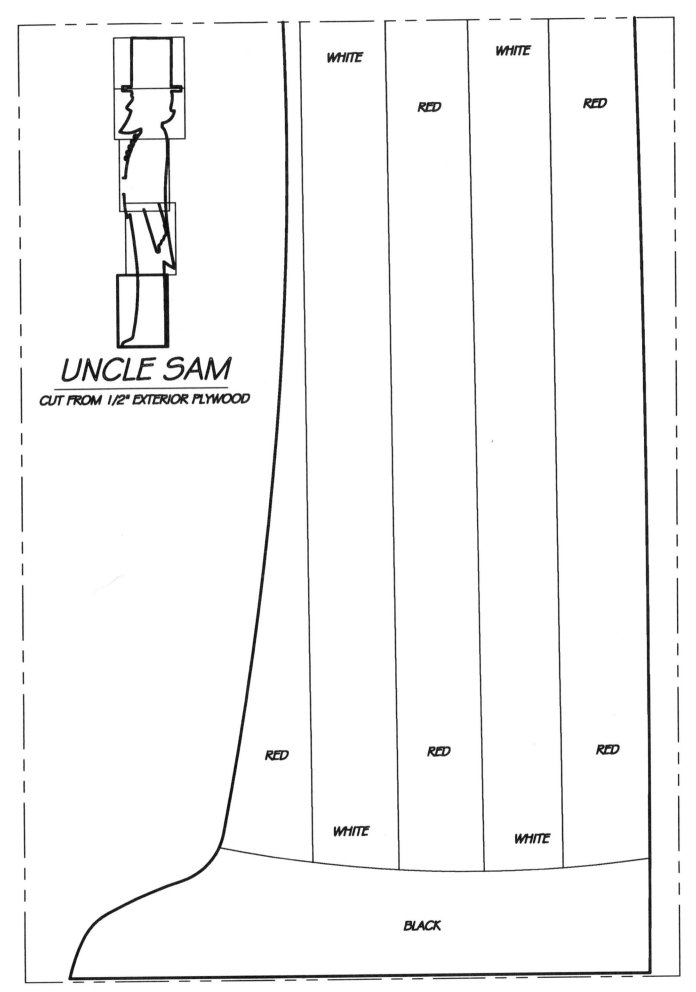

UNCLE SAM

CUT FROM 1/2" EXTERIOR PLYWOOD

WHITE

WHITE

RED

RED

RED

RED

RED

RED

WHITE

WHITE

BLACK

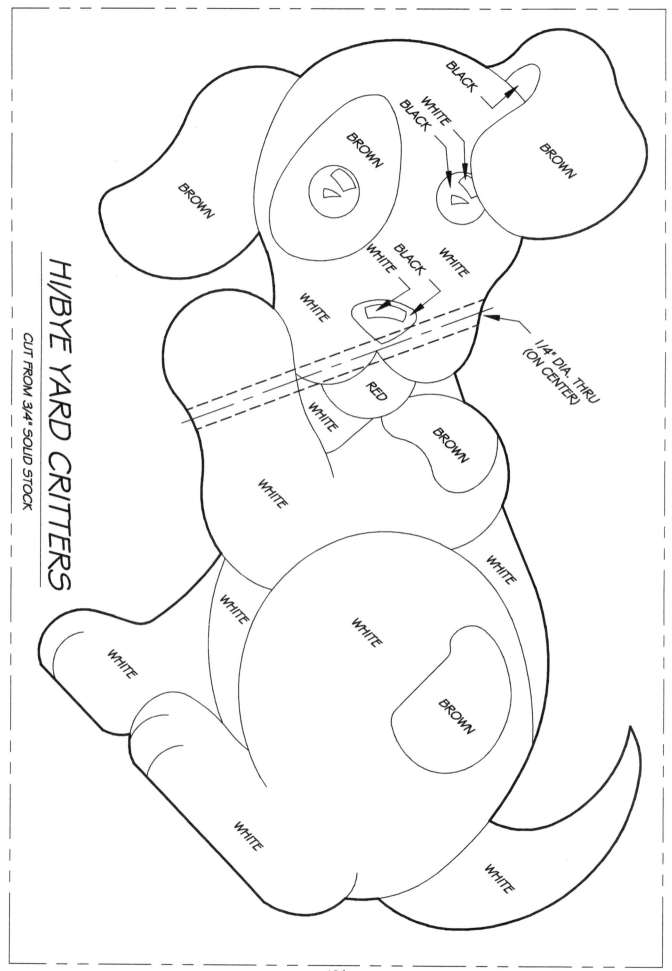

HI/BYE YARD CRITTERS

CUT FROM 3/4" SOLID STOCK

BLACK

WHITE
BLACK

BROWN

BROWN

BROWN

WHITE

WHITE

BLACK
WHITE

1/4" DIA. THRU
(ON CENTER)

RED

WHITE

BROWN

WHITE

WHITE

WHITE

WHITE

BROWN

WHITE

WHITE

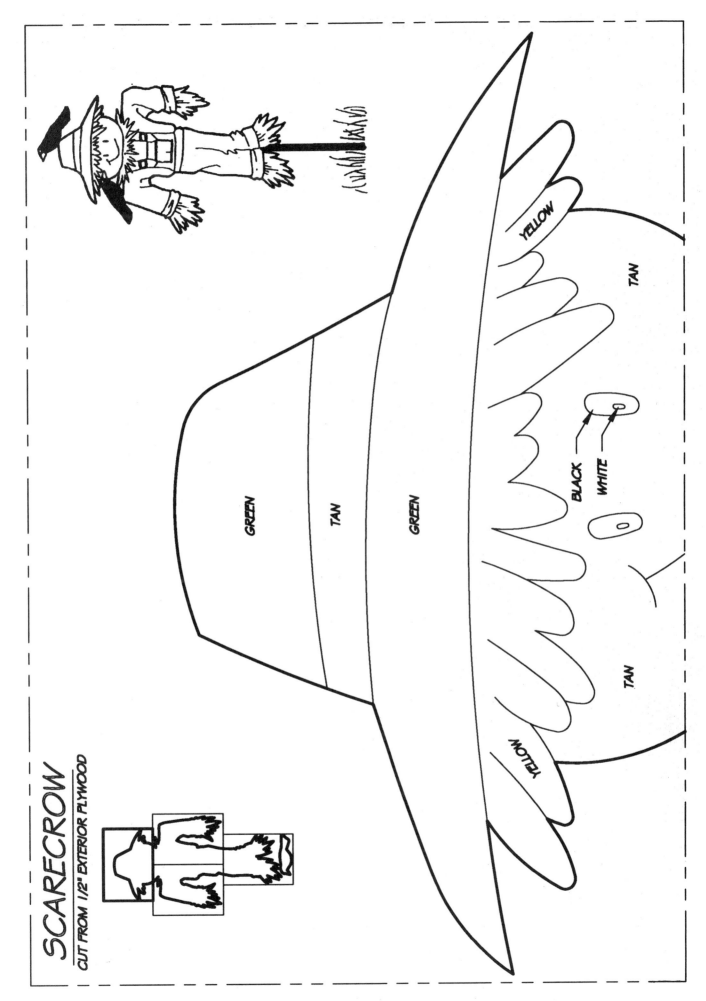

SCARECROW
CUT FROM 1/2" EXTERIOR PLYWOOD

GREEN

TAN

GREEN

YELLOW

TAN

BLACK

WHITE

YELLOW

TAN

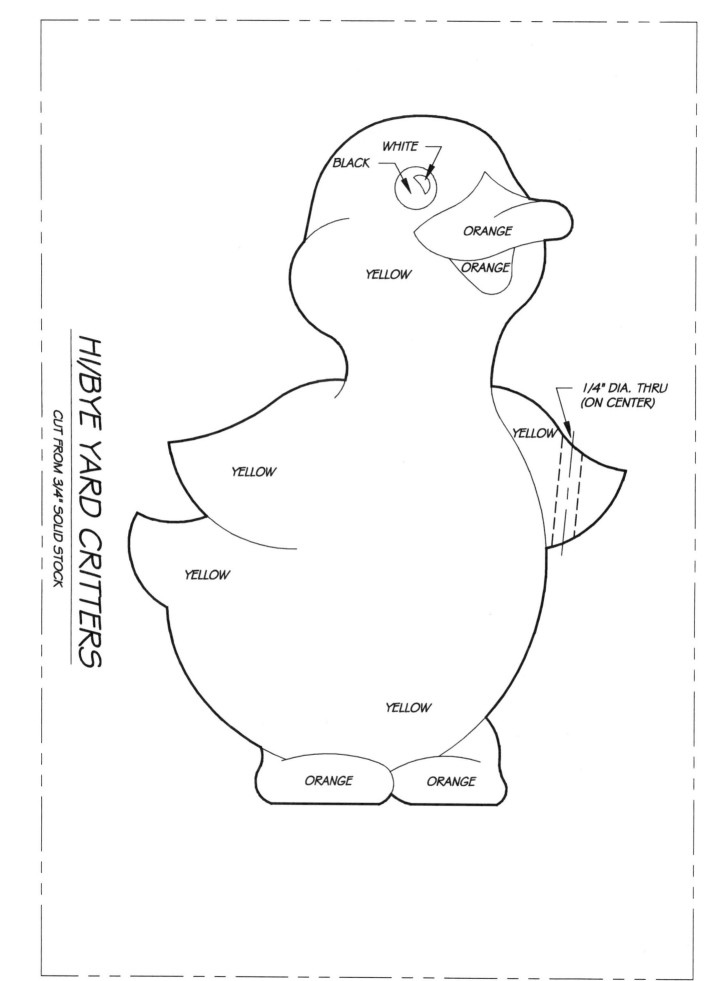

HI/BYE YARD CRITTERS

CUT FROM 3/4" SOLID STOCK

BLACK

WHITE

ORANGE

ORANGE

YELLOW

1/4" DIA. THRU
(ON CENTER)

YELLOW

YELLOW

YELLOW

YELLOW

ORANGE

ORANGE

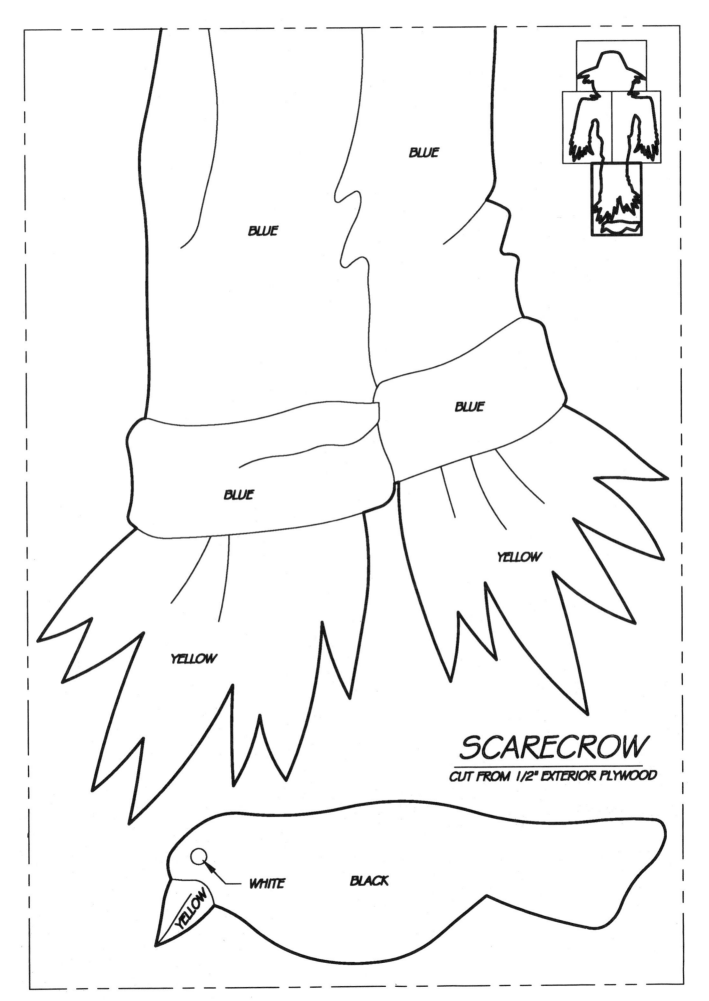

BLUE

BLUE

BLUE

BLUE

BLUE

YELLOW

YELLOW

YELLOW

SCARECROW

CUT FROM 1/2" EXTERIOR PLYWOOD

WHITE

BLACK

YELLOW

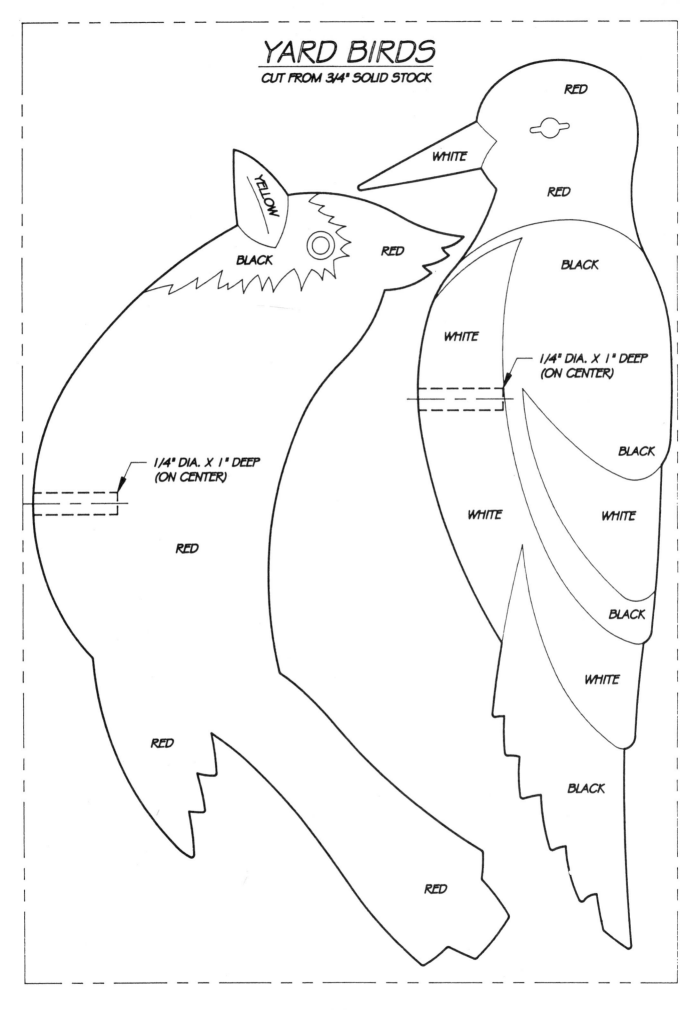

YARD BIRDS

CUT FROM 3/4" SOLID STOCK

RED

WHITE

RED

YELLOW

BLACK

RED

BLACK

WHITE

1/4" DIA. X 1" DEEP
(ON CENTER)

1/4" DIA. X 1" DEEP
(ON CENTER)

BLACK

WHITE

RED

WHITE

BLACK

RED

WHITE

BLACK

RED

RED

About the Author

Paul Meisel's experience in woodworking and design is extensive. During his 10 years as an industrial arts instructor, Mr. Meisel realized the need for project plans that the beginning woodworker could manage. He began designing projects that excited interest in students, yet did not exceed their skill level.

Realizing the need for well-designed plans for the school as well as the home-hobbyist woodworker, he and his wife, Pat, set about creating a mail order company for the distribution of these plans. They took their unique concept one step further, by offering many hard-to-find specialty hardware parts. This company, Meisel Hardware Specialties, has become one of the nation's leading project plan and woodworking supply companies.

Their company has published plans for over 2,000 woodworking projects, all of which feature Mr. Meisel's rigid criteria for simple, practical construction. He's dedicated to providing fresh ideas each year with a focus on clean, straightforward designs that create maximum impact, while using common sizes of lumber and simple painting and finishing techniques. He specifies materials and power tools that are readily available to the do-it-yourselfer.

He has received numerous awards for his woodworking projects. Many have appeared in books and magazines. In addition to his woodworking and design interests, Mr. Meisel is an accomplished writer. While pursuing his doctorate, he researched the area of educational gaming and published numerous games in the mid-1970s. Most of these games are still being marketed nationally. Based in part on his experience as a shop instructor, he published over 20 booklets in the area of technology education and has also written books on designing and creating board games, chemical safety, and measurement. In 1993, Mr. Meisel co-authored a book with Patrick Spielman titled *Country Mailboxes*.

Acknowledgments

This book would not have been possible without the help and cooperation of many people. I would like to give a special thanks to the following:

For furnishing pictures, ideas, or suggestions:
Becky Easton, Carnation, WA
Ruby and Larry McCurry, Jonesboro, TN
Leroy Miller, Johnson City, IN
Dan Wallace, Topeka, KS
Carl W. East, Hurt, VA
Ed Franzese, Lincoln Park, NJ
Emmett Johnson, Superior, WI

For help with layout, proofing, photography, props, illustrations, drawings and plan development:

Boyd Emerson	Bob Pearson
Sheryl Gerlach	Daryl Peterson
Dale Hamer	Carol Pomeroy
Chris Larson	Melanie Rieschl
Michael Luethmers	Peter Schermer
Pat Meisel	Kim Truax

For valuable technical assistance:
American Plywood Association, Tacoma, WA
National Paint and Coatings Association, Washington, D.C.
Paint Quality Institute, Wheeling, IL
Wm. Zinsser and Co., Inc., Somerset, NJ